Trouble
With
Boyfriends

Tricia Kreitman worked as a psychologist, designing sex education programmes for young people, and then as a psychosexual therapist before becoming a full-time author and broadcaster. She has been an advice columnist for eighteen years, specialising in young people's and women's problems, and she is currently working with *Blush!* magazine and the BBC World Service. A parent of teenagers herself, Tricia was a director and then Chair of Brook Advisory Centres for young people for six years. She is also an experienced TV and radio broadcaster.

Tricia has published widely in the general medical and lay press and her previous books for young people include *Everything You Ever Wanted to Ask About . . . Periods* and *Everything You Ever Wanted to Ask About Willies and Other Boys' Bits.*

The Trouble With Boyfriends

TRICIA KREITMAN

Piccadilly Press • London

This book is for every girl who turns to the problem page first in her favourite magazine

First published in Great Britain in 2003
by Piccadilly Press Ltd,
5 Castle Road, London NW1 8PR

A catalogue record for this book is available from the British Library

ISBN: 1 85340 773 9 (trade paperback)

1 3 5 7 9 10 8 6 4 2

Printed and bound in Great Britain by Bookmarque Ltd
Typeset by Textype Typesetters
Cover design by Fielding Design

Set in 10.5/16pt Futura Book

Contents

Chapter 3 – Are Boys Really From a Different Planet? 57

Acknowledgements

I'd like to thank all the young people who helped me with this book.

Particular thanks are due to (the wonderful) Viki and her friends, Ginny, Elli, Gwen and Rachel, who encouraged me by brainstorming problems; to Jane Dale and the lower sixth students (particularly L6D) of Queen Elizabeth's Grammar School, Horncastle, Lincolnshire, who answered endless personal questions with great good humour; and to all the other boys who allowed themselves to be persuaded to give their point of view.

Introduction

There's no doubt that young people today have access to much more information about growing up than their parents ever did. In fact, many of them are probably better informed than their parents are now! But that doesn't mean that those same young people don't also have problems and worries, for which it can be very difficult to find answers. In a major study by a UK teenage helpline, it was found that relationships were the single biggest worry facing young people. Scoring way ahead of drugs, unwanted pregnancy or bullying, this result came as a shock to many parents and other adults. We all know that it can be difficult or embarrassing for young people to discuss personal relationships with their parents (often the parents themselves can be part of the problem), but this survey result comes as no surprise to anyone who has worked with and listened to teenagers.

I originally trained as a psychologist and relationship counsellor, but I have been an advice columnist (more commonly known as an agony aunt) on teenage magazines for the last eighteen years. Contrary to what most people believe, the problem letters in these magazines are very real and I often receive up to two hundred a week. Many do ask for information about the practical aspects of growing up, but – and these are by far the most distressing to read – a large proportion are from young people who are struggling with relationship difficulties.

This book is based on typical examples of these problems and each chapter follows a particular theme, with questions and answers on that topic. Reading it, you might think that all girls have problems with boyfriends. But remember that people without problems rarely write to agony aunts!

Each chapter also has quotes from real boys talking about their point of view – something they don't often share with girls! At the back of the book, there's a Contacts section with telephone numbers and websites for information and support on many of the different problems that girls – and their boyfriends – may encounter.

I didn't write this for parents or adults – although they might be interested to see the kinds of problems it deals with. Instead, I wanted girls to know that they're not alone when they worry about their relationships and how to juggle them with the pressures of friends, parents, school and exams. Most of all, it's about understanding what makes a good relationship great and finding the courage to get out of a bad one before it turns into a disaster area.

Tricia Kreitman

Chapter 1

Could This Be Love?

How can I tell if he likes me?

I really fancy this guy at school, but I'm not sure he even knows I exist. Whenever I try to talk to him I clam up and feel myself go red. How can I tell whether I stand a chance?

If this boy was just a friend, you'd have no problem smiling and chatting to him. But, because he isn't and your heart lurches whenever you see him, you become tongue-tied and shy and too scared to open your mouth. You need to take a step back and analyse the situation. Does he show any signs (however slight) that he might be interested? Does he ever smile or watch you as you go by? Does he say hi or even look as though he's about to? Does he go pink and look away if you smile at him? If you don't know the answer to these, treat it as an experiment. Give him your best friendly smile and see what happens!

Maybe he's already aware of you and is too shy to do anything about it. Perhaps he hasn't even noticed you. Either way, your best chance is to seem open, friendly and definitely non-threatening.

How can I get him to talk to me?

There's a boy in the year above me who keeps staring at me. We've danced together a couple of times at school discos and now he often waves if he sees me around. But he never speaks, even though I'm dying for him to ask me out. Do you think he likes me and, if so, what can I do about it?

Trust me – he's definitely interested! He's paying attention to you, waving and making it as plain as can be by dancing with you when he gets the chance. The major snag, of course, is that he's just as shy as you. So you need to encourage him. Take it slowly, but wave and smile back whenever you see him and, most important of all, try saying something. It doesn't much matter exactly what you say because the important thing is to break the silence. You don't need to ask him out or anything; just get talking to him. Once he feels comfortable with that, he's far more likely to ask you out himself.

Boys Talk!

What do you find most attractive in girls?

Looks, figure, hair colour, personality (probably).
Jack, 17

Funny, intelligent.
Leify, 16

Looks, sense of humour, intelligence.
Cortez, 17

Good attitude with a bit of looks. Intelligent, funny.
Stretch, 17

Smile, eyes, lisp – don't ask me why!
Daniel, 16

Intelligence, nice nature, humour.
Geez, 17

Good looks, open, chatty, generally good fun to be with. However, the whole playing-hard-to-get thing is really off-putting.
Mick, 16

Initially her looks, and then her personality once you get to know her better.
Max, 16

Funny, outgoing personality, friendly, flirty.
Jay, 17

Interesting to talk to (not boring), good-looking, short.
Tim, 17

Girls that fancy you are always attractive!
Tom, 16

First impression would be looks, but having a good personality is definitely just as important.
Mixu, 17

I like people I feel at ease with, with whom I'm friends. Being close to someone always makes them seem attractive.
Anon

Intelligence and kindness are more important than looks.
Fred, 17

Good personality, sense of humour.
Joe, 15

How can I tell if he's serious?

The boy I like keeps texting me and sounds really keen, but he never seems to want to talk to me. If I ring him up, he makes an excuse and gets off the phone, and if I go up to him at school, his friends all start nudging each other and laughing. It's really irritating because I don't know whether he likes me or is just winding me up.

Tricky! It could just be that he is shy and his mates are all making fun of him because they know he likes you. But, because he never talks to you in person, you can't be totally sure the texts are from him alone and not from the whole group of them giggling over his mobile. No wonder you're annoyed and confused. Somehow you have to give him the message that you'd be happy to talk to him (without his mates), but you're no longer interested in playing any text games. Tell him face to face, ring him (you can say it in the thirty seconds before he puts the phone down) or send a text yourself. But – and this bit's important – after that you must stop responding to his texts. Make it clear that if he wants to make contact he's got to do it in person.

I fancy my best friend's ex

My best friend's been going out with a boy for six months, but recently they broke up. I've always liked him and now I can't get him out of my mind. I want to ask him out or at least go round and see if he's OK, but I'm scared it will upset my friend.

There's a very important rule of life here: best mates should always come before boys. It's not that boys aren't wonderful, exciting and totally worthwhile human beings in their own right. It's just that, by the law of averages, you're likely to go out with more boys than you'll ever have best mates. And, when you're first getting to grips with them, relationships with boys tend not to last very long, but fall out with a long-standing best friend over a boy, and you may never get her friendship back.

Never make a move on a friend's ex until you've sounded her out about it first. If you can't imagine asking her, it probably means you know she'd be really upset. Tempting as it may seem to pop round and see if he's OK, you and I both know that's only an excuse to try to get closer to him. Be honest here. Put your friend and your joint friendship first for a while and give her pain a chance to wear off. You already know this guy and if he's keen on you, it will eventually happen anyway.

Is it OK to go out with my ex's best mate?

I broke up with my boyfriend because things just weren't going anywhere. He accused me of seeing someone else (which wasn't true) and got very upset. He's calmed down now, but I realise that I'm very attracted to his best mate. We used to spend a lot of time together as a threesome and now I miss him. Would it be OK to ask him out?

The same rule applies as in the question above. It's not fair to risk breaking up your ex's friendship until he's had a chance to cool down. And, if his best mate really is his best friend, he won't want to do anything yet either. The future's another story and you have the enormous advantage of already knowing and liking each other.

Boys Talk!

What do you find least attractive in girls?

When they just won't stop talking.
Jack, 17

Muscles.
Leify, 16

Being loud-mouthed.
Cortez, 17

Someone who thinks she is God's gift to mankind.
Stretch, 17

Moody girls, girls who talk non-stop, girls that drop hints that they like you but don't really.
Daniel, 16

Selfishness.
Jon, 17

I don't mind if a girl is shy, but if it's impossible to hold a conversation with her I would probably stop fancying her. Also, if she or her friends made fun of me I would stop.
Nick, 16

Non-feminine actions.
Justin, 16

Boring conversations, irritating behaviour.
Max, 16

Dyed pink (or similar garish colour) hair. Snobby, no sense of humour, boring.
MacKenzie, 16

Annoying voice or laugh. Boring conversations, arrogance, if they think too much of themselves.
Tim, 17

Gobbiness, narrow mindedness, sluttishness, lack of effort.
Tom, 16

Having an attitude or bitching about friends.
Mixu, 17

A self-centred attitude or talking behind people's backs.
Henry, 17

Lack of personality and interests. It feels like the wheel's going, but the hamster's dead!
Anon

Arrogance, mood swings, uptightness.
Jay, 17

Tarty, lots of make-up, bossy.
Joe, 15

When they fancy themselves a bit much.
Dom, 16

I'm scared of getting hurt

I'm fifteen and have never been out with a boy. It's not because I'm shy or don't get asked out; it's just that I've seen so many friends get badly hurt that I'm scared to fall in love.

Now I've met someone who I get on with well and can't get out of my mind. The snag is, he's very popular, a great flirt and has a reputation for two-timing. He's asked me out and I don't know what to do. My friends keep telling me how much he likes me, but I'm so afraid of being hurt.

Going out with anyone for the first time is bound to make you feel anxious and nervous, but if you're really terrified, or it feels totally wrong, then you shouldn't be doing it. It might be that you simply aren't ready for a relationship yet. Being fifteen has nothing to do with it, because everyone matures at their own pace and pushing yourself into something too soon is bound to end in disaster.

On the other hand, you could be the sort of person who always tries to avoid risk. Playing safe is often very sensible, but many of the most exciting things in life, including growing up, having relationships and eventually falling in love, involve some degree of risk. Asking someone out carries a risk of rejection. Falling in love makes you totally vulnerable because the other person's feelings may not run as deep. You can never guarantee how someone else will respond, but you only need to take one step at a time. He's asked you out – it isn't an invitation to elope to a desert island – nor should you feel pressured to do anything you aren't ready for. The worst that can happen is that one of you will be a bit of a disappointment to the other. Embarrassing, certainly, but hardly the end of the world.

If you think he's worth it, give him a chance. Take your time and listen to your intuition. If he treats you badly, be prepared to walk away at once with your head held high.

Should I pretend I have a boyfriend?

I've never had a boyfriend, but all my friends are really experienced. All they ever talk about is boys and who they're seeing. I feel very left out and I know they think I'm odd. I'm tempted to make up a boyfriend and pretend he's someone from out of school who they'll never meet. However, I'm scared I'll get found out. Would it be totally pathetic to make one up just to avoid the hassle from my friends?

I can understand the temptation and I'd be willing to bet you wouldn't be the first of your friends to do it. Peer pressure is very powerful and many girls do invent boyfriends or, even worse, rush into damaging relationships just because they don't want to feel left out.

The snag with making up a romance is that your friends will want to know more and more details and, unless you're a brilliant storyteller, they'll eventually smell a rat. Why not just say that you've got your eye on someone very special who they've never met. Be mysterious and refuse to answer questions for fear of tempting fate. Your time will come – just don't let their boasting get to you too much in the meantime.

Boys Talk!

What worries you most about asking a girl out?

Humiliation.
Cortez, 17

Finding out the girl you like is already secretly going out with your best mate.
Jon, 17

That she would laugh in my face and say no, while everyone else laughed at me too.
Dustin, 16

All your friends being around seeing you make a fool of yourself.
MacIntyre, 17

For her to laugh and call me pathetic or something along those lines.
Martin, 16

If she laughed at me.
Will, 16

Her simply not replying and then blanking me.
Rob, 17

Saying something that would hurt her and getting it all wrong.
Jay, 17

She might laugh or tell me to grow up!
Joe, 15

What's the worst thing that ever happened to you when asking a girl out?

I always, but always, make a fool of myself.
Jack, 17

I went out with a girl for two weeks and we never spoke! I kept thinking something would happen, but it never did.
Anon

I once asked a girl out on the phone, then ignored her for the whole of the next day because I was so embarrassed.
Joe, 15

I asked a girl out in front of a lot of classmates on a ferry to France, but it was worth it because later she said yes.
Dustin, 16

I had what I was going to say all planned, but I panicked a bit and started stuttering.
Dom, 16

I stuttered and said stupid, dumb things.
Tim, 17

I was drunk and threw up next to her!
Henry, 17

I said stupid things without meaning to because I
was so nervous.
Jay, 17

I don't like kissing – is there something wrong with me?

I'm really embarrassed at the thought of having sex or even kissing anyone. I'm nearly sixteen and have never had a boyfriend, but recently on a school trip I sort of got off with a guy, mainly as a dare. When we kissed I just felt really squirmy and couldn't wait for it to end. Is there something wrong with me? Am I a lesbian or do you think I'm just not ready for any of this?

Sexual attraction (and that includes interest in romance) is largely driven by hormones. And, just as girls mature at different ages and some develop long before others, it can also take longer for some girls to feel any interest in boys. Being naturally shy or coming from a family where anything to do with kissing or sex is seen as embarrassing can make it harder to find the confidence to start a relationship. Getting off with someone as a dare isn't exactly the best start! There's no reason to think you're a lesbian unless you're having feelings towards other girls. When you do meet the right person (of either gender) kissing and touching will seem natural and your doubts will vanish.

I think I'm gay, but I can't tell anyone

All my friends ever talk about is boys, but I know I am not like that. I have always had crushes on girls or women and the idea of being with a boy – and kissing him – makes me feel physically ill. I know this probably means I'm gay, but I can't tell anyone and I don't know what to do about it.

It's common to have strong crushes on people of the same sex as you grow up. You're looking for role models – people you can admire and love. You may just be a late developer when it comes to boys, but for some girls, these feelings grow stronger as they get older until they realise they are sexually attracted to women rather than (or as well as) men. There is nothing wrong with this, even though many people are still uncomfortable or embarrassed at the idea of same-sex relationships. Telling friends and family how you feel can be difficult – particularly if you're not sure of your feelings yourself. Talking this through with someone you can trust will help a lot and I'd suggest contacting one of the confidential helplines like

ChildLine or Sexwise in the first instance. Have a look at the Contacts section for other sources of information and support.

I like him, but I'm scared to kiss him

I keep sort of going out with this lad at school. We really like each other, but he's dumped me now three times because I won't kiss him. We hold hands and stuff, but it isn't enough for him. I'm very shy and mainly I'm scared to kiss him in case I do it wrong. What should I do?

Kissing (with the right person) can be fantastic, but there's no point even trying unless you feel you want to. Doing it because you're worried about being dumped isn't a good enough reason! It sounds as though this boy is putting pressure on you. This will only make you more nervous. Can you talk to him about it? Tell him how much you like him, but ask him to ease off and give you time. If he cares for you, he will.

He won't snog me

I went to a party with a whole group of my friends and a boy that I've liked for a long time was there too. I knew he was interested and I went to a lot of trouble to look great, thinking that this would be the night. He kept looking at me, but still I had to make the first move so I asked him to dance. That was fine until the slow dances when everyone else was snogging. He just wasn't interested and eventually said he had to go home early so I was left like a lemon. I called him up the next day and asked what the matter was and he said just to forget it. I asked if we were going out, but he laughed. I feel so let down and I don't understand what's wrong with him.

You probably feel frustrated and angry and maybe a bit humiliated. You'd planned the evening and gone to a great deal of trouble, but this boy simply wouldn't play his part. That's the trouble with love. You can't write other people's lines for them.

Perhaps he's got a secret girlfriend or just doesn't fancy you. Or maybe he isn't ready to start any kind of relationship yet. Pushing him isn't going to help. Despite what you may hear, not all boys are desperate for sex – they can be shy too and would often prefer to wait until they feel sure about things. Chasing after him won't change anything. Keep it friendly for a while and, however much it hurts inside, hold your head up and try to pretend you aren't upset.

Boys Talk!

How do you feel before going out with someone for the first time?

Hopeful and slightly hungry.
Jack, 17

Nervous.
Leify, 16

Anxious.
Cortez, 17

Nervous, but excited.
Stretch, 17

I really don't like to go out with people unless I'm really sure about it because it's so easy to make a mistake.
Nick, 16

Apprehensive. Worried about making a good impression.
Dan, 18

Horny, excited, kind of nervous.
Tom, 16

Worried, nervous, but also excited that it could lead to greater things.
Henry, 17

Anxious, wanting to make a good impression without making a twat of myself.
Anon

Excited in anticipation – but also nervous and a bit sick.
Jay, 17

Should I risk going out with my best friend?

I've known this boy forever. We're the same age and really close. We can talk about everything, but I was still gobsmacked when he asked me if I'd go out with him. My immediate reaction was to say no because I was so scared it would ruin our friendship. He took it OK and isn't going out with anyone else, but now all I can think about is how much I like him.

How can I tell him and would it be a disaster if we did go out?

There's no way it wouldn't affect your friendship – but it could be for the better and many great romances start out like this. You know where you are with him. You trust him and you wouldn't have all those early relationship crises about whether he really likes you or not (well, probably not so many anyway!). The dilemma is, of course, if you eventually break up. Realistically, most teenage relationships don't last forever and handling the break-up is much harder than coping with the early stages of romance. If you lost him as a boyfriend you might lose him as a friend – at least for a while. That would leave you very lonely, but if your basic friendship is strong enough, you should eventually be able to get over that and resume friendly relations.

If you can't tell him straight what's bothering you, try the not-so-subtle method of commenting that sometimes you could kick yourself for refusing his offer. If that doesn't work, drop a few hints about how you wish other boys were as nice as him.

I think I've ruined our friendship by asking him out

I've been close to this boy for ages and, when I realised how cute he was, I found the courage to ask him out. He said no and then it was like he disappeared off the face of the earth. I never see him and he makes excuses not to speak if I call. The trouble is, I still really like him, so how can I get him to notice me again? Even better, how can I get him to go out with me?

You may have frightened him. Even if he's now regretting having refused you the first time, storming in and asking him out again will only terrify him. He's probably embarrassed by the change in your relationship and that's why he finds it so hard to talk to you. You need to give him some breathing space and concentrate on letting some of that basic friendship re-grow. Whenever your paths do cross, smile and be friendly. Even if he doesn't say anything you can still make it clear that what happened wasn't the end of the world. With time – and luck – he'll get over his fear and the way forward will be easier.

How can I tell him I love him?

We've been going out for eight months and I know that I'm totally head over heels in love. The thing is, we're both quite shy so I don't know how to tell him that I love him.

The trouble with saying those three little words is that they can so often sound like a question. You say 'I love you', then there's that horrible pause while the other person has to decide whether or not they are ready to say it too. You can avoid that (a bit anyway) by telling him at the end of a phone conversation, just before you put the phone down, or by waiting for a romantic moment – for example, looking at the stars at night – or just as his team scores the winning goal. As you throw your arms around each other, just tell him how you feel. Then carry on counting the stars, cheering or whatever.

If he isn't ready for this yet and looks panic-stricken or desperate to break away, you can laugh it off as something you said in the heat of the moment. Not necessarily very honest, but a bit safer than an all-out declaration of love.

Chapter 2

Friends, Family and Interference

My friends asked him out, but he won't give an answer

I have the feeling that the boy I'm interested in also likes me. He always smiles at me. I wanted to ask him out, but I was too scared so my two best mates offered to do it for me. They went up and told him that I liked him and asked if he'd go out with me, but he just said that he'd think about it. Since then nothing's happened. Should I get them to ask him again?

No way! Using best mates as go-betweens in this situation is a cop-out. You know this guy, so you're already on smiling and speaking terms. You got them to do the asking because you were scared of being rejected. He won't commit himself for exactly the same reason. He does sound interested, but he's probably also shy and may not be able to believe that you are as keen as he is. Being faced with two giggling girls supposedly asking him out on your behalf has got to make him wonder if it's a wind-up. In other words, he's scared you'll all laugh at him. There's nothing else for it. You're going to have to talk to him yourself!

Should I trust my friends' advice?

I'm really good at giving my friends advice if they like a guy and they always turn to me like an agony aunt or something. But in my own life I never seem to get it right, even when my friends warn me and tell me what I should be doing. I know I should try and trust them more and take their advice, but it's so difficult when they say one thing and my heart says another.

Tell me about it! You give good advice to your friends because you are able to stand back and be objective about their situations. However, when it comes to your own life, all your emotions and feelings get in the way. You could have as easily said that your heart says one thing and your head says another. And good friends who act as your head and keep you on the straight and narrow in times of temptation – or protect you from people who are downright dangerous – are invaluable.

Of course, not all friends always get it right or have your best interests in mind. Think hard about whom you can trust and then resolve to listen to their words of wisdom, weighing them against your own feelings, next time you're at risk of making a dodgy decision.

My friend's told everyone I like him and now he won't talk to me

I'm madly in love with my older brother's best mate. He comes round to ours a lot and is usually really nice to me. Now I can't get him out of my head and I made the mistake of telling my best friend. Suddenly, the whole school knows. I'm not ashamed of how I feel, but my brother says that everyone's teasing his friend about it and he doesn't like it. Now he ignores me when he comes round and my brother has even suggested that I should stay out of his way for a bit.

As I said in the previous answer, not all friends always have your best interests at heart! Maybe it was a slow week for gossip or something, but it just shows how hard it is to keep a secret. But then maybe a part of you wanted everyone to know . . . Did you think it might push him into liking you? Well, unfortunately it hasn't worked.

There's nothing you can do about it for now. But you have at least got the advantage that, because he's your brother's mate, you will have a chance to see him. Don't push it – just stick to being friendly. If anything, play it cool. Give the idea a chance to take root in his mind and, if he does like you, maybe he'll act on it.

Should I believe what my friends say about him?

I've just started going out with a new boyfriend. I don't know him very well, but lots of his friends know lots of mine. I think he's great, but now some of my mates have been telling me that he slags me off behind my back and often laughs about me with his friends. They keep saying I should dump him, but I don't want to. I've asked him about it and he denies everything, but now I'm finding it hard to trust him.

Do you think it's possible there are too many people in this relationship? How much of your distrust and unease is based on Chinese Whispers? Who do you trust most? Is there a chance that your friends (or his) are just trying to cause trouble? Or are some of your really close friends saying things that are likely to be the truth?

Forget about what 'everyone' says. Choose someone you do trust, a close friend or even your mum, and talk it through with them. That should give you a clearer idea of how you feel. If you do decide to carry on, stay alert for any first-hand signs of boy behaving badly. That way, you can make a quick exit before you get seriously hurt.

Boys Talk!

How important would it be to you what your friends thought of your girlfriend?

I don't care because it's my decision who I go out with and no one else's.
Damian, 17

Not important, but I would want them to like her.
Anon

I'm sure if I liked her, then they would too.
Joe, 15

If I like the girl I don't really care, but I know how difficult it is to keep a relationship going if my friends don't get on with her.
Nick, 16

I need to know my friends approve of her, but that's it. It's between you and her – not your friends. But if they hate your girlfriend, it would make it very difficult.
Max, 16

I would like them to like her, so we could go out with her friends and my friends, but it isn't that important.
James, 16

Not very, though from experience it is hard going out with someone your friends don't like, particularly if those friends are female. Blokes don't normally seem to care.
Rob, 17

Fairly important, but it shouldn't get in the way.
Anon

I think there is a certain amount of influence from what your friends think. I wouldn't want to be picked on.
Will, 16

If they hated her it would influence me, but I could live with it.
MacIntyre, 17

Important, but not so important that it would affect us.
Dan, 18

It would matter because I would like them to get along, but both relationships can be kept separate if necessary.
Daniel, 16

Not that important at all. As long as I'm happy with her, that's all that really matters.
Ian, 16

I'd like my friends to like my girlfriend because I trust their judgement, but it wouldn't matter that much.
Anon

It depends how important the girl is to you. If she was really special it wouldn't matter.
Joe, 15

Not very because if I like her, why should I care?
Dom, 16

I want him back, even if I lose my friends!

I have two close friends and we all fancy the same boy. He's a year older than us and really, really popular. I actually went out with him a few months back, but it didn't last, though now I'm convinced that it could work. The only thing is, if I ask him out, my friends will go ballistic. But I can't think of anything else, so do you think it's worth the risk?

Are you sure you don't want to go out with him just because he is 'really popular'? Remember, he isn't a prize for the prettiest or most cunning girl – but someone who can do their own choosing when it comes to girlfriends. And if it didn't work before, why should it have any more chance this time?

You can't predict how he'll react, but you can be sure that your mates will be furious. If the two of you are meant to be together then it will happen, but try not to tread all over your best friends on the way.

My friends were jealous of my boyfriend

I was the first one of our group to get a proper boyfriend. At first my friends were all very supportive, but then they started to complain that I never spent enough time with them. Soon I began to feel left out because they'd organise things without me. One girl in particular was really nasty and eventually told me they all hated my boyfriend and that I had to choose between him and their friendship. I tried to explain to her that it wasn't that simple, but in the middle of all this, he suddenly dumped me. The next thing I knew he was going out with her! My mum says I should have seen it coming, but she was a really good friend and he was a great boyfriend. I miss them both. What can I do?

You've certainly been in the wars! It's a good thing you can talk to your mum about this because you must be feeling angry, disappointed and hurt. There are two issues to consider. Firstly, jealousy between friends and boyfriends. This happens a lot. Sometimes they may just be jealous of you having a boyfriend and want one (perhaps even yours) for themselves. But they can also feel neglected if you suddenly spend all your time either with your boyfriend or wittering on about how wonderful he is. That's why it's important, always, to make time for your friends – however desperately wrapped up you are in your new romance. So, next time you fall in love – and you will, try to be more tolerant of your friends and avoid that problem.

But the second issue is best mates who stab you in the back like this. It does sound like she was the ring-leader and certainly took on the role of persuading you to give him up. Whether or not she always planned to get him for herself is hard to say, but if she really is your friend, she ought to listen when you tell her how much this has hurt you. Try talking to her alone about it if you can. She may try to shrug it off as nothing, but if she does value and respect you, it should put her off ever acting like this again.

As for the boy, I can only echo what your mum has probably already told you. If he goes around acting like this, he isn't good boyfriend material anyway.

He got off with my best friend behind my back

I had to miss a party because I was ill, so my boyfriend went alone. My two best friends were also there, supposedly keeping an eye on him, but they all had a lot to drink and one of them got off with him. I only found out because there was a love bite on his neck. When he eventually told me what had happened I confronted my friend and she admitted it. I'm really angry with all of them and I don't know what to do.

You must feel betrayed and left out. You're having a crisis with your boyfriend and, just when you need them, your two best friends have completely let you down. No wonder you're furious with them. You have a right to tell them how angry you are. Hopefully the girls will understand how much they've hurt you and your friendship will be strong enough to forgive them this one mistake. Good friends are hard to come by and usually not worth losing over a cheating bloke.

A few strong words are also due to your boyfriend. Some boys are easily flattered, to the extent that they find it hard to resist any attractive woman who throws herself at them. Nevertheless, any guy with more than half a brain would think twice before getting off with a girl's best mate.

Boys Talk!

Do you think a girl's friends have a big influence on her relationship with a boy?

Depends on the girl. Some it would, others it wouldn't.
Damian, 17

Yes, peer pressure persuades girls to act in different ways.
Daniel, 16

Yes, if a girl's friends don't like you, the girl will be less likely to choose you over her friends.
Jon, 17

Definitely. I know I may be a bit biased, but I feel that sometimes her friends have more control over the relationship than she does.
Nick, 16

Yes, if friends don't like the lad they will pressure the girl.
John, 16

Girls talk to each other so much, so you know they'll discuss you and she can't help but be affected by what they think of you.
Charles, 17

Yes — girls always gossip about boys and always want their friends' opinions. What's more, they listen to their advice!
Jay, 17

Would you make an effort to get on with your girlfriend's friends?

Yes, but not if they annoyed me.
Steve, 16

Only if they were willing to get on and make friends with me too.
Jon, 17

Yeah, always. I hate falling out with people.
Nick, 16

I would treat them the same as other people, but wouldn't go out of my way just to get on with them.
David, 17

I make an effort to get on with her friends, but sometimes it just doesn't work.
Max, 16

If they're fit. You never know what will happen when you break up!
Charles, 17

Yes, if her friends are as important to her as mine are to me, then it's vital for a healthy relationship.
Nick X, 17

Yes, otherwise her friends might discourage the girl from seeing you.
Henry, 17

You have to really, because you end up being around them such a lot.
Rob, 17

Yes, because it would be important to her and you want to get closer to her.
Jay, 17

Yeah, if they were supportive of her going out with me.
Joe, 15

My friend keeps stealing my boyfriends

I've known my best friend since primary school. She's much prettier and more popular than me, but it still seems that anything I have, she wants. She's already gone out with a boy that she knew even before she set eyes on him I really, really liked. Then on a school trip I met someone else and started seeing him. She kept saying how nice he was and flirting with him. The next thing I knew she'd told him I was about to dump him (which absolutely wasn't true) so he finished with me instead. Guess what? She immediately asked him out.

How can I ever trust her again?

Are you trying to qualify for sainthood? Look, there are little mistakes and there's being treated like dirt and I know which is happening here. This girl's obviously wracked with jealousy and insecurity. She's not so much trying to steal what you have as attempting to keep from you anything that makes you happy. She has real problems and if this goes on she'll alienate anyone who gets close to her. Maybe she needs to hear that. Possibly you're just the person to tell her!

If you want to give her another chance, spell it out very clearly that you'll never, ever put up with anything like this again. A friendship is nothing without trust and you're clean out of that at the moment.

How do I tell my family I have a boyfriend?

I've never had a proper boyfriend, but my family are always teasing me and asking me who I like and who I'm seeing. Now I have started sort of going out with a boy at school and he wants to come round and see me at the weekend. I'd like that, but I've got no idea how I'd introduce him and it really worries me how my family would react.

Well, you could try saying bluntly that he is 'just a friend' and ignoring any of their teasing comments, but you'd probably only end up blushing and giving the game away. It would be better to get one person, preferably your mum, well briefed beforehand. Say you need her help and explain that you like this boy and you're 'sort of going out', but that you're worried about everyone laughing at you. I'm sure she will jump to your defence and be only too pleased when you say he'd like to come round at the weekend. Of course she's going to want to give him the once over, but it's much better to get that over and done with as soon as possible. Letting your mum into your confidence means she's more likely to keep an eye on the rest of them for you and, in particular, smooth the way with your dad who's bound to be very protective of his 'little girl'.

When your boyfriend does come round, introduce him simply by saying, 'Mum, this is John', and then add something about him (for example, where he lives or what his hobbies are), so there's an easy topic of conversation to break the ice. Have an escape route ready. Say you're going for a walk together in the park or something, but reassure her that you'll be back later for a cup of tea. This gets you out of the house easily and gives your mum and everyone else a chance to calm down.

Make sure you warn your boyfriend about this plan in advance, but he should be pleased to cooperate because it will make the ordeal less traumatic for him too!

My family tease me about my boyfriend

About three weeks ago I started going out with a boy I've liked for a long time. He's lovely; he rings me up most nights and we talk for ages. At the weekend we went out on my first 'proper' Saturday date and he came to pick me up from the house. Unfortunately my family (mum, dad and two brothers) think it's hilarious and they tease me every time he rings. They went on and on about meeting him until I was so embarrassed that I ran out of the house as soon as I saw him come up the street. I hate it when they act like this, but they don't seem to understand how much it upsets me.

The sad thing is that most parents probably complained about this when they started dating too. Grown-ups, even loving mums and dads, can be surprisingly insensitive. What you have to remember is that they're probably embarrassed too. This is your first proper boyfriend and it makes them realise that they're a stage closer to losing their little girl. It may also make them feel their age! Their teasing is a clumsy attempt at humour to cover up their own uncomfortable feelings.

Get your mum on your side. Choose a moment when the two of you are alone and say you'd like to ask for her help. This should arouse her protective, maternal instincts and you can follow up by telling her how difficult you find it when everyone has a go at you about your boyfriend. I know you'll probably blush and feel very awkward, but that will help get the message over to your mum. My guess is she'll feel very sympathetic and do her best to calm the others down. Apart from that, try to ignore them. They're the ones being silly and the novelty will soon wear off.

Boys Talk!

How would it feel meeting your girlfriend's parents for the first time?

I'd feel really nervous about making a good impression.
Joe, 15

OK. I get on well with people, but I'd be a bit worried about the father.
Daniel, 16

Nervous as you'd be trying to make a good impression so they approve of you.
Jon, 17

I always mess it up because my nerves get the better of me. I end up sounding mouthy and cocky, but I'm not like that really!
Ben, 17

It's a bit intimidating and nerve-wracking because you want to show them you're responsible and so on.
David, 17

I'd be worried as to whether they approved of me and I'd probably try so hard to make a good impression

I'd end up making a fool of myself.
Tom, 16

If I could manage it I would try not to meet them as it would be extremely scary.
Anon

I would be nervous as hell! I'd try to be polite without seeming like a brown nose.
Anon

Nerve-wracking because you're so conscious of what they might think of you.
Jay, 17

Truly scary!
Dom, 16

My mum won't give us any privacy

Whenever my boyfriend comes round my mum hovers about, offering us cups of tea and things. I'm not allowed to take him into my room, so we end up either in the kitchen with everyone else coming in and out, or in the front room knowing that she and the rest of the family are probably listening outside. It's as though she doesn't trust me and I really resent it.

It's probably not so much a matter of trust as fear. This is about sex! Even if she won't admit it, your mum is scared that you and your boyfriend will get carried away and 'go too far'. But she probably feels embarrassed talking to you about it – almost as embarrassed as you do discussing it with her. However, unless you *do* talk about it, the situation is going to go on and on. Rather than having a go at her, try telling her, calmly and clearly, how you feel, and that you want her to know you are very aware of the risks, and that you have no intention of doing anything stupid. This may lead to a tricky, or even illuminating, birds-and-bees discussion, but it will clear the air. Your mum might also be reassured to hear that you would ask her for advice if you ever had a problem or worry.

I met this guy on the internet and my dad won't let me meet him

I got talking to this guy in a chatroom and we've been emailing ever since. He sounds great and it's really cheered me up knowing that he cares about me. He's asked lots of questions about where I live and things, but never made me feel uncomfortable. Recently he gave me his mobile number and we started texting as well. I'd like to talk to him properly, but he always makes an excuse. However, he has now suggested that we should meet and is planning to come and see me at half term. The trouble is my parents found out and my dad went ballistic. He said that I'm not allowed to see anyone I meet over the internet and, if necessary, he'll ground me. What can I do?

I can understand why your dad is so worried. The internet is fantastic and lots of people make great friends and even fall in love through it, but, you have to admit, it's also very easy to present yourself as something you're not. Look at the facts here. This guy is friendly and caring and is keen to push your friendship further by meeting face to face. But, in the meantime, he won't speak to you on the phone. That makes *me* suspicious, never mind your dad!

Sadly there are far too many cases of men posing as young boys on the internet and 'grooming' children and teenagers in the hope of eventual sex. I know you're convinced your friend isn't like this, but how do you know he really is who he says he is? Be honest and tell him that your dad is concerned. Say there's no chance of you meeting unless you at least start talking on the phone first. That will give you a better idea of his age. Then, if you do want to go ahead and meet him, you have to do it with your dad's permission. That will mean making sure you have someone with you when you do meet – whether that's at your house or somewhere more public. If things don't feel right or it all goes wrong, you could need help to get away from him. I appreciate that doesn't sound very romantic, but your safety is the most important thing here. If this boy is for real, there will be no problem. Let's hope it is the start of a beautiful friendship.

My parents don't approve because he's older than me

My boyfriend is four years older than me and my parents are convinced that he's 'only after one thing'. I know he really cares for me and he isn't putting any pressure on, but how can I get them to accept that?

Parents do worry; it's part of their job description. The only thing that will help is time and some friendly cooperation from your boyfriend. You need to give them a chance to get used to him. Rather than always spending time out, try to get him included in some family occasions, like a Sunday lunch or Granny's birthday tea. Get him to pop round now and then, not to take you out, but just to be friendly and have a cup of tea in the kitchen and chat to your mum. Give them a chance to see him treating you well and they'll start to feel more at ease.

My parents say I can't have boyfriends

My parents are very strict and say that I can't have a boyfriend until I'm eighteen and have left school. I know this is ridiculous because all my friends have boyfriends, but they just won't listen. Should I go behind their backs?

You know this would only cause more trouble. If you got caught, and sooner or later you would, they would lose all trust in you and life would become even more difficult.

You have to take this one slowly and try to prove to them that you are sensible and willing to listen to them. It would also be useful to find out what their biggest worry is. If it's a cultural or religious position, then it could be very hard to change their attitude, but if it's based on fear for you, patient discussion and negotiation should gradually win you more freedom. The important thing is that you always do what you've agreed to do. For example, you're back at the right time and you're with the people you said you were going to be with. Getting caught lying or letting them down will send you back to square one.

Boys Talk!

What's it like introducing a girlfriend to your family?

Awful. My dad would make fun of her.
Jack, 17

Worse than death.
Leify, 16

A bit scary. I'd be worried the family might not like her.
Steve, 16

Easy. My parents are very understanding.
Daniel, 16

Think of hell meets elevator music. Baaaad!
Bruno, 17

Hard, I'm part of a large family and with three brothers they might give me a hard time.
Jon, 17

I'm usually proud of my girlfriends so that doesn't bother me. Also my family are very easy to get on with.
David, 17

It depends on the girl in some respects. If they have a good, talkative personality I wouldn't be worried, but if they are shy I get nervous and feel sorry for them.
Tim, 17

OK, because my parents are cool and I have a good and honest relationship with them.
Nick, 16

I live with my dad and he just makes jokes so it's not too bad.
Robbie, 17

It's very scary!
Dom, 16

I'm worried about meeting his parents

I'm going to meet my boyfriend's parents for the first time and I'm really scared. He's been to mine quite a bit and that wasn't too bad, but he gives me the impression that his mum in particular will make a big thing of it. I know I'm his first serious girlfriend, so I suspect he's nervous too. How can I make sure it goes off OK?

Boys are often much less socially skilled about this than girls, so it's good that you've already realised he's a bit nervous. Be prepared for the fact that he may not have told his parents much (or anything) about you. This isn't a reflection on how he feels for you, just the way that boys often act. As a result, he may try to hurry the whole process so that you get whisked in and out of the house without much of a chance to say anything at all. However, if you want to make a good impression it's important that you do seem friendly and open. Make a point of saying hello to everyone and try and follow it up with a compliment about the colour of the kitchen, his mum's cooking or whatever. Even if you sense your boyfriend edging out of the door, try to keep chatting for a few minutes. Apart from guaranteeing their approval, it sets a very good example to socially challenged boys!

My boyfriend hurt me and now my mum won't let me see him

I went out with my boyfriend for nearly a year and I thought we were really in love. Then, out of the blue, he ditched me in the most hurtful way possible and it took me forever to get over it. My mum was great – really supportive – but absolutely furious with him. The thing is, he's now told me that he's sorry and wants to start seeing me again. Even though he hurt me so much I still love him and I do want to give it a second try, but my mum won't hear of it and has banned me from having any contact with him.

Your mum was there for you when you were at your lowest. She saw exactly how badly you were hurt. So you can't blame her for wanting to protect you now. This boy did treat you badly, but, with an apology and a few nice words, seems to have won you over again. Getting back together would be taking a risk. And, if you did get hurt again, it would be better to have the sympathy and understanding of your mum to fall back on, wouldn't it? So, if you're really determined to see him you should try to do it with her understanding, instead of behind her back. Rather than making demands, try to have a grown-up discussion with her about what happened and why she's so worried now. This will be painful for both of you, but it will help you move on to a more equal relationship where you can negotiate for more freedom. You'll also have to make it clear to your boyfriend that he needs to tread carefully with both you and your mum. If he really wants you back then maybe he ought to come and say that to her himself. If he's serious, he'll give it a go.

His parents keep going on about his 'perfect' ex

My boyfriend's parents make it very clear that they don't like me. His mum 'pretends' to forget my name and keeps making comments about his ex-girlfriend who was supposedly wonderful. It makes me so angry, but I don't want to get into a row because I know it would only make things worse.

Turning the other cheek is definitely the best policy. This sounds like some kind of power game, and I suspect his mum is jealous of you. She can see how much he likes you and resents you for it. Perhaps she really is absent-minded, but getting your name wrong is a very effective way of hurting you and dropping comments about his ex-girlfriend is just as sly. Remember that 'ex' is the operative word here. He's going out with *you* now, even if you aren't his mum's first choice. Be polite and don't let her get to you.

My religion means I shouldn't see him

I'm a sixteen-year-old Asian girl and I really like a boy in our year at school. My friends all say he likes me too and that I should go for it. I'd love to, but I'm scared of getting caught. He isn't our religion and my parents would never allow it.

I know all your friends are encouraging you and trying to be matchmakers, but you know you have to be very careful to make up your own mind here. Unless your friends share your culture and religion they're unlikely to understand the way you've been brought up and the values your parents expect you to live by.

No one can pretend this is easy for you, because in many ways you probably have far more freedom than your parents ever did. But you know that going against their beliefs could cause serious and long-term problems, possibly even cutting you off from your family forever.

It would be helpful if you could speak to someone who understands your position – perhaps an elder sister or aunt? It should be someone you trust and have respect for. The free and confidential helplines, Get Connected and NSPCC (see the Contacts section at the back of the book) can also help, and may be able to recommend local support for someone in your situation. Remember – you've done nothing wrong and these feelings are normal.

Chapter 3

Are Boys Really From a Different Planet?

Do boys and girls have different brains?

I never know where I am with boys! One minute everything can seem normal, as though you really like each other, and then they start acting all weird. Is it that boys don't grow up as fast as girls, or are their brains really completely different?

Boys definitely are different to girls, but that may have as much to do with the way they've been brought up and how the world expects them to behave as with any actual physical differences in the brain. Research shows that people speak and behave towards babies and toddlers differently according to which sex they are. Boys are encouraged to be more noisy and boisterous. Girls, on the other hand, are praised for being quiet and neat. It's not surprising that this affects how you grow up. Boys also tend to start puberty later than girls, so can still be at the giggly, embarrassed stage when girls are ready for a more serious relationship.

That being said, girls tend to have better connections

between the two sides of the brain, allowing them to be aware of and to express their emotions more clearly and be more creative when it comes to problem-solving. Boys are often more talented in the logic department and more focused on taking action, rather than mulling over a problem, looking at it from different angles.

Look at what happens when a girl or a boy is feeling depressed about a relationship problem. A girl will usually talk it through with her friends. They will sympathise and offer examples of similar problems they've had. Hearing about these makes the girl feel understood and supported. On the other hand, if a boy tells his friends about a similar problem (and that's a big if) they might look embarrassed or try to change the subject. If a close friend does try to say anything constructive it's likely to be along the lines of, 'Dump her' or 'Tell her to get real' – action-based rather than sympathetic and emotion-based.

Sharing personal problems and emotions helps bond groups of girls together. Often boys form bonds by watching football games together and getting excited about their team's performance, or talking about practical subjects like computers or motorbikes.

Of course, these are generalisations and it would be wrong to say that all boys or girls act in any one way. However, understanding the differences can help you cope with and enjoy relationships with boys better. Remember, boys get equally confused about the female sex as we do about them!

He never wants to spend time alone with me

We've been going out for six weeks and we talk most nights on the phone, but we never get to see each other on our own. At school there are always people around and, when I suggest doing things out of school, he either makes excuses or brings his friends along. I end up feeling embarrassed and often go home and leave him to it. I don't understand why he's like this.

If the two of you are really able to keep long conversations going on the phone night after night then this relationship must have something going for it! My bet is that he's shy and worried about saying or doing the wrong thing when he's alone with you. Perhaps he's concerned about taking things too fast or too slow, or scared he won't be able to kiss you properly. He's certainly using his friends as a safety blanket and your only chance of breaking through his defences is to tell him how you feel.

Make it easy for him. Rather than demanding that the two of you have a cosy night on the sofa, announce that you just *have* to see the latest film and you've already booked tickets for the two of you. If he's really as keen on you as he sounds, he'll be relieved that you've taken the matter out of his hands!

Do boys really only like quiet girls?

I find it amazingly difficult to get guys to be interested in me once they realise I'm pretty articulate. I can be mates with them, but beyond that they're just not interested. Grown-ups and friends say I should wait for someone more mature. I know this is a sensible idea, but I never get to meet new people. What can I do?

Many educational experts think that boys mature more slowly and that's why, particularly in junior school, it can be so difficult for teachers to teach both sexes together. Girls often want to get on with doing their work carefully and neatly, while boys are more interested in rushing around making a noise and playing the fool.

Girls often start puberty earlier as well and when boys are surrounded by capable, achieving and obviously more mature girls, it's not surprising they can feel threatened. It may well seem that they prefer quieter, less articulate girls, but research suggests that what boys look for most of all in a potential girlfriend is openness and a friendly personality. After all, if you're feeling threatened, you're more likely to talk to someone who smiles and seems approachable.

The people you've spoken to are right; this situation will resolve itself as you get older, but in the meantime, you could help boys out by giving them more chance to talk about themselves so that they're not just listening to your views on the world. You don't have to go all shy and girly, just remember that sometimes they need drawing out. It's hard to do this when they're in a group, but in fact most boys find it easier to open up on a one-to-one basis.

Boys Talk!

Do you find it easy to tell if a girl likes you? If so, how?

Yes, they tell you.
Jack, 17

Yes, because if a girl likes me she'll seem to be more friendly.
Steve, 16

No, it's never easy to tell.
Tim, 17

To be honest, it's only if they're quite open, otherwise it's a mystery.
Nick, 16

Yes, her attitude towards you is more to please you and hints are sometimes made about her liking you.
David, 17

Everyone's different. Not all people express their feelings as well as others, so with some people you can tell if they like you and some you can't.
Max, 16

Yes, they always hang around you and never give you a moment's peace!
Mick, 16

Yes, eye contact, body language, facial expressions and so on.
Dan, 18

Yes, they start paying you much more attention and are more flirty.
Tom, 16

Sometimes. People tell you, i.e., their friends let you know, and the girl stares!
Mike, 17

Sometimes – their friends tell me or their friends tell my friends.
Henry, 17

No, I normally assume they're just being friendly.
Rob, 17

In some cases. They make an effort to talk to me and laugh at my jokes.
Paul, 17

No – only if they make it really obvious by flirting.
Joe, 15

Why does he treat me differently when we're with other people?

I've started going out with a boy from school. We've been friends for a long time but only really got together at the end of the holidays. When I see him at school he acts like normal and, to listen to him, you'd never think we were boyfriend/girlfriend. When we're on our own he's lovely, but I always feel unsure of where things stand between us because of the way he treats me at school.

He's probably just as confused as you. Maybe he's one of the first of his friends to have a girlfriend? Perhaps his friends already know about you, or at least suspect the two of you are together, and are teasing him about it. They might be jealous, and that makes it very difficult for him to make any public show of affection for you.

Girls are much better at talking about feelings than boys. For example, I expect you've already discussed this problem with your friends, but boys feel more comfortable with less emotive subjects. As soon as more of them have girlfriends it will be easier for him to talk about you in that way, but until then, it's just too hard for him to open up about something that seems so personal.

He acts like this because of the way he feels with his friends – not because of how he feels about you. Try to understand this, but do tell him how uncomfortable it is when he virtually ignores you. Perhaps the two of you could find an occasion, like a school disco, when you could be publicly 'together'. Once his friends have seen and accepted you as a couple, life will be much easier.

Boys Talk!

How would you like a girl to let you know she's interested in you?

Tell me and be to the point about it.
Damian, 17

Just be straightforward.
Al, 16

Quietly, personally and in confidence.
Daniel, 16

Talk to me herself rather than getting her friends to do it.
Jon, 17

I'd prefer it if girls were more open about things like that. If they conceal a lot, I don't feel like doing anything, because I don't want to make a fool of myself.
Nick, 16

Just let you know by any means – friends, to your face, by text or whatever.
David, 17

Telling you personally rather than telling someone else.
Max, 16

Be flirtatious, touchy-feely.
Tim, 17

By coming up to me, preferably when I'm on my own, and saying so.
Rob, 17

Say something to me rather than wait for me to work it out.
Paul, 17

To make eye contact and flirt!
Jay, 17

Neither of us knows what to say!

I'm an only child and I've been going out with my first boyfriend for nearly a month. He goes to an all-boys school and doesn't seem to have much idea of how to talk to girls. I'm quite shy and haven't had any experience with boys to speak of so, although I think we like each other a lot, it does lead to very awkward silences. We usually meet up after school and end up walking around the park, watching boys play footie or something. We've been to a couple of films, which was good because it gave us something to talk about, but apart from that it's really difficult. To make matters worse, he sometimes makes quite sarcastic comments. I don't think he means it and he always apologises afterwards, but it's upsetting and nerve-wracking at the time.

It's sometimes much easier to make conversation with

people you're not strongly attracted to! You're both nervous and trying to make your best impression. Unfortunately, under this kind of pressure, it's easy to say the wrong thing or say the right thing in a horribly awkward way. Like many other shy people, his comments can come out as sarcastic and biting. He must realise this, so it's not surprising he's reluctant to say much at all.

Luckily, there are a couple of things you can do to help. Try admitting to him how shy you feel and how difficult you find it talking to boys. Hopefully this will encourage him to open up a bit and admit his own shyness. Once you've acknowledged that you have this in common you can start laughing about it.

Secondly, you can practise the very useful conversational skill of asking open-ended questions. This means any question that can't be answered with a direct yes or no. Get him to tell you about his friends. What do they look like? What are their interests? Once you've got a picture of them, you can encourage him to fill you in on the latest gossip. And you can do the same for him. It's not the most romantic of conversations, but it helps you both feel at ease and builds links between you. Encourage him to open up on anything he feels passionate about. You may never have realised how fascinating table football or stamp-collecting could be!

He never rings when he says he will

My boyfriend drives me mad because although we get on well when we're together we can only usually meet up at weekends. He always says he'll call me during the week but never does. When I call him he's pleased to hear from me, but I don't understand why he can't keep his promises.

You have to understand that time passes differently on Planet Boy! He says he'll call you and he means it at the time, but to him there's no great importance. He knows you'll still be there and he'll see you next weekend whether he picks up the phone or not. It's a much bigger deal to you because you're worrying that he's gone off you or is trying to make a point by not ringing. Admittedly, boys do sometimes dump girls by simply breaking off contact (see the next letter), but if everything else seems to be going well, you probably just need to relax a bit. Without making it into a row, try talking this through with him so that you can understand each other's point of view more clearly. And then stop calling him so much. Give him a chance to miss you!

If it's over, why doesn't he tell me?

We've been going out for three months. I thought everything was fine, but all of a sudden he's started avoiding me at school and he doesn't answer my texts or calls. I've tried asking him what's wrong and he just says he'll talk to me later. But he never does. My friends say I'm wasting my time and that he's dumped me. I just want to know what's going on.

I can understand your frustration, but I suspect your friends are right. For reasons of his own, he's decided that your relationship is over. In fact, he's already moved on in his head so he doesn't feel particularly connected to you. Of course, he knows he ought to tell you, or at least try to explain what's happened, but that means having to deal with emotions – yours as well as his. He's taking the lazy and cowardly way out and there's not much you can do about it. You've already tried cornering him, so perhaps you should write him a note or a text saying that, unless you hear back from him, you assume the two of you are history. This won't change much because you're unlikely to get any response, but it might make you feel a bit more in control of the situation.

We're supposed to be going out, but I never see him

I started going out with this boy two months ago, but because we're at different schools, we don't often meet up. We speak on the phone a bit, but whenever I try to arrange something it never seems to work out. My mates all say I should finish it because he isn't worth it, but I don't know what to do.

'Going out' with someone implies a bit of commitment and action on both sides. From what you say, you're making all the effort and he's just making excuses. It may be that he just wants to have someone he can call a girlfriend, but isn't actually ready for a relationship. Or perhaps he is looking for a way out or never really considered there was anything very serious between the two of you in the first place. If he won't talk about it, try avoiding him for a couple of weeks. Don't phone or text. If he makes the effort to contact you, then you're in with a chance, but if he stays silent, you'll know it's over.

He thinks it's funny when he calls me names

We've been going out for four weeks, but I feel uncomfortable because my boyfriend often makes fun of me. He says things about my skin and hair. I find it really upsetting as I have slight acne. When I've told him I don't like it, he says I should be able to take a joke. I know he doesn't mean it, but what should I do?

He may not mean it, but it's still hurting you. The problem is that he's used to making these sort of 'jokes' with his friends, who all feel perfectly comfortable doing the same to him. Now he's trying to handle a relationship with a girl and he thinks the same approach will work. You have to tell him again that you find it hurtful and upsetting and not funny. Try pointing out that you worry a lot about your appearance, so find it hard to take what he says as a joke. If he cares for you and has the maturity to try to curb his behaviour, then things should get better. If they don't, then the only way to show him this isn't acceptable may be to tell him it's over.

Boys Talk!

What do you find most confusing about girls?

Their obsession with the size of their bottom.
Jack, 17

Mood swings.
Chris, 16

Their constant complaining.
Steve, 16

It's so hard to tell what they want or what they're thinking.
Al, 16

Why they want to see me so often if we're going out.
Will, 16

Why they cry all the time. And the way they bitch at each other.
Daniel, 16

Their insecurity.
Henry, 17

The way they always go round in big groups. You can never get them on their own.
Jon, 17

Their whole thought process.
Mick, 16

Everything they do and their mood swings. Do they put them on sometimes? Or are they always due to periods?
David, 17

The way their thought processes are completely different to ours!
Max, 16

Knowing whether they're really interested in me and also how many double standards they set for us and everyone else.
Tim, 17

The way they talk about nothing for long periods of time.
Robbie, 17

Why two girls who've never met hug each other if they're crying.
James, 16

Why do they take so long to do their nails?
Ben, 17

They contradict themselves and demand too much, yet when you give them what they want, they moan

that you're being obsessive!
Nick, 16

Mixed signals, changing their mind about you really quickly and then ignoring you. Why is this?
James, 16

The way they need to know everything about everybody.
Bas, 17

Constant mood swings and believing that men can mind read!
Paul, 17

Why do they fall out with their friends so much over really stupid things?
Phil, 16

They often seem to have a hidden agenda about which I don't have a clue.
Dom, 16

He sulks but won't talk about the problem

We've been going out for five months and although we're close, my boyfriend has a real problem with jealousy. I keep trying to reassure him, but every so often he gets the idea that I've been over-friendly with another boy and goes into a major sulk. I try to get him to talk about this, because even a row would be better than silence, but it's as though he's closed himself off totally. How can I break through?

People express anger in different ways. This is partly due to their personality, but also a result of the way their families dealt with anger while they were growing up. For example, someone whose parents were always having screaming rows may either have a very hot temper themselves or find it extremely hard to show anger because of the fear they felt when their parents were rowing. Boys also often find it harder to express their emotions in words so may act things out rather than discussing the problem and trying to negotiate a solution.

Your boyfriend is jealous and wants to punish you for making him feel like this. Sulking and shutting himself off from you is his way of doing it. In fact it acts as a very effective control because you feel rotten and go out of your way to talk him round. Unfortunately this isn't very healthy and, in some relationships, it can shift the whole balance so that one partner is constantly trying to persuade the other out of the sulk.

Jealousy is destructive, but, assuming you aren't really messing around with other boys, it is his problem and something that he has to deal with. Try discussing this at some time when he isn't sulking, making it very clear how close he is to destroying your relationship. Ask him how he would recommend you react when he goes into a sulk. You might be surprised at his response – and it could help a lot. If he has real problems with anger and jealousy, then they'll cause difficulties whoever he's with. In this case he should consider getting help from a helpline or counsellor. See the Contacts section for suggestions.

Boys Talk!

What would you like girls to do differently?

Not dye her hair blond.
Steve, 16

To stop complaining.
Al, 16

Be more straightforward.
Anon

Be upfront with you and not discuss your relationship with their friends so much.
Joe, 15

Be more honest.
Daniel, 16

Make more decisions for themselves.
Jon, 17

Be more individual and see outside their friendship groups.
Nick, 16

Be more positive in flirting.
Mac, 17

Compliment me – a lot!
Tom, 16

Be more open about what they feel.
Phil, 16

Be more honest and faithful.
Henry, 17

Be more open and change their minds less. In some cases they could be a lot less manipulative too.
Rob, 17

Mud wrestle!
Jack, 17

To be consistent and know what they want (so that's probably not possible!).
Paul, 17

Be straight to the point without playing games with you. Be more forward – even 'wear the trousers' sometimes.
Jay, 17

My boyfriend looks at porn on the internet

I'm disgusted because I found out that my boyfriend has been accessing pornographic websites on the internet. I thought at first it was just a joke, but when I looked at the history on his computer I couldn't believe it. What's more, he admitted it and doesn't seem to think there's anything wrong with it. We've just started having a sexual relationship and now I don't want him to touch me. I can't understand what's wrong with him.

This is a very common problem between the sexes. Many men (and nearly all young men) are fascinated by and use pornography – at least occasionally. Before the days of the internet this usually meant top-shelf men's magazines being passed around furtively behind the bike sheds. Now anyone can access porn and it's often much more hardcore and brutal than anything in the average lad's magazine.

Boys like it because it plugs straight in to their sexual response system. They get turned on and they often use it to masturbate. But for most of them, although it's obviously sexual, it's much more like scratching an itch than having a relationship with a woman. They would see the two as totally separate. That's why your boyfriend can't understand why you're upset.

Nonetheless, you have every right to explain to him how this makes you feel. Point out that while he may find it a turn-on, it has the opposite effect on you and you don't want him to touch you after he's looked at it. Accepting that boys like and use porn may be difficult, but try to understand that he is different to you and is being honest when he says that what he looks at on the computer doesn't affect how he feels about you. But you can, if you want, warn him that if he *must* use it, it could well affect your feelings for *him*.

We never talk, so is he just using me for sex?

I know it sounds crazy, but although we've been going out together for nearly six weeks I don't feel as though my boyfriend and I have ever had a chance to get to know each other. We met when we got off at a party and whenever we're together all he wants to do is snog or take things further. I enjoy that too, but we never seem to talk and it's now got to the stage where it's almost embarrassing because if we're on a bus or in public together there's nothing we can say to each other. Do you think he's just using me for sex or is this a normal relationship? My friends all say that he'll dump me if I try to slow things down now. What should I do?

You fancy him, he fancies you, so when you start kissing and touching each other all the everyday questions about school and family go out of your mind. At the moment you're more in lust than in love. This means a lack of communication can be dangerous. For example, if you're going to have sex he could get into trouble if you are under sixteen and you are at real risk of sexually transmitted infections (STIs) and pregnancy if you haven't been able to sit down and discuss risks and protection.

Lots of boys find it hard to chat, and action (in this case, snogging) comes easier than discussing feelings. But that doesn't mean that talking isn't a vital part of a relationship. You're scared of taking a stand on this in case he dumps you, but unless you do, you're not going to be happy with him. At the moment he doesn't bother because he thinks you're OK with things, but if he does care for you, he will be able to cope with a bit of talk time. The obvious route is the phone. Maybe he doesn't feel very comfortable using it, but try encouraging him.

Speaking together, particularly late at night, is very intimate and he may find it easier to start talking about his feelings. Try suggesting some things you could do together, like walking in the park or running an errand for your mum. Give yourselves a chance to feel comfortable together without being glued at the lips. Encourage him to open up by asking his advice – for example, what options does he think you ought to choose at school? This may not be very sexy, but it's non-threatening and will give you a chance to find out who you're really going out with.

Chapter 4

Crisis Management

I can't keep relationships going for more than a few weeks

Although I've had several boyfriends, nothing ever lasts longer than a few weeks; three months was my absolute record. It's always my fault. It starts out OK, but it's too good to last. I begin noticing things that annoy me or start to obsess about why he didn't call when he said he would. I know I pick silly rows and get very moody and none of the boys I've met have been able to handle this. I really like my new boyfriend and I don't want to mess it up this time round. What can I do?

Maybe you haven't found the right boy yet and each relationship has simply run its natural course. But, if your suspicions are correct, you could be subconsciously sabotaging relationships before they get too serious. The question is: why? It's possible that you're scared of being close to a boy because of something that happened to you in the past – maybe you had a bad experience? If your problem is low self-esteem and self-confidence (also frequently linked to events when you were growing up) you may feel at a subconscious level that you don't deserve a loving relationship. Starting squabbles and throwing moodies might be your way of testing the boy because you can't believe he really cares for you. Of course, by being so difficult, particularly so early in a relationship, this belief becomes a self-fulfilling prophecy and the two of you split up.

Understanding what's happening is the first step. Breaking the pattern can be much harder and it could help to talk to a specialist relationship or young people's counsellor about this. At the very least, try discussing it with a close and trusted friend, or use the Contacts section at the back of the book to look for further help.

He gets off with me but won't go out with me

I've liked this boy for years, but now it's getting serious. The awful thing is he doesn't feel the same way. He's at school with me and whenever we're at parties he's really flirty and we end up dancing and snogging. Nothing else has happened yet, but I think I would go further if he asked me. Lots of my friends have got serious boyfriends and I've asked this boy out loads of times. He never exactly says no, just that he'll think about it. But then he never mentions it again.

I think I'm falling in love with him and I don't understand whether he feels the same way. What can I do?

The bottom line here is that you want more than he is prepared to give. He likes you, he enjoys flirting with you and would be very happy to take things further. But it doesn't sound as though he's ready to have a committed relationship yet.

What's more, as long as you make yourself freely available to him any time he feels up for it, there's no reason why he should change his mind. You have to learn to say no to him. If he wants to know why, explain you're looking for a real boyfriend not just someone who fancies a quick snog on a Saturday night. If you can't trust yourself to say no, ask one of your friends to watch out for you and dig you in the ribs if you get too close to him.

Ignoring him at parties may not have any effect. If he genuinely doesn't understand about emotional relationships (or isn't ready for them), then he'll just find someone else to flirt with. But if it's really you he's interested in, he will eventually make an effort.

I'm in love with my parents' best friend

I'm sixteen and for the last two years I've babysat for my parents' best friends' kids. They're a great family and sometimes I go for the weekend to help with the kids and I really enjoy it. The thing is I'm growing closer and closer to the father. He's the same age as my dad (almost), but is very good-looking and always takes time to listen and talk to me. He doesn't treat me like a kid at all. I think he knows how I feel because he always makes sure it's him who drives me home afterwards and recently he's started stopping the car on the way back so that we can have some time on our own together. I don't want to break up their family, but I'm sure there's something special between us.

I'm really worried about you. You've obviously developed a massive crush on this man and no one can blame you for that. But I do blame him for encouraging it and putting everyone's happiness at risk by starting to take things further. He's not only married with kids, he's also your dad's best friend and is therefore in a position of responsibility towards you. Flirting with you simply isn't acceptable. Taking things any further than flirting would be a catastrophe.

Few men are immune to flattery and adoration from a young girl and he is obviously no exception. But that doesn't excuse him. Men often fantasise about flirtations like this, but they rarely leave their wives and split their families up over them. It is girls like you who end up with their hearts broken! You have to get yourself away from him. I know it's the last thing you want to do, but you must start making excuses not to be alone with him. Ask your dad if he can pick you up or get busy with a project for school so you haven't got time to babysit for a while. With luck he'll get the message and mend his ways.

I'm worried he'll dump me because I don't look like a pin-up

My boyfriend's nearly two years older than me and on his bedroom wall he has lots of posters of naked women – usually with amazing figures and enormous breasts. It's not so much that I mind them being there, but I'm sure he's always comparing me to them. I'm quite short and a bit plump and I've been trying to lose weight, but there's no way I'm ever going to look like one of his pin-ups. It's really depressing and I'm scared he'll dump me.

You're feeling bad about yourself, so the question is – where is this coming from? If it's only you comparing yourself to the pin-ups then you're in a no-win situation. There probably is no way you'll ever look like them – but then very few women do (or not without cosmetic surgery or a lot of clever photo enhancements). They may be on his wall, but he's going out with you. Try telling him the pictures make you feel uncomfortable – and, if necessary, explain why. Perhaps he's not very good at paying compliments, but sometimes actions speak louder than words.

If, on the other hand, he is saying things that directly compare you with them, then you're the one who ought to be thinking about doing the dumping. A boy who doesn't take any trouble to make you feel good isn't worth having as a boyfriend. If you want to give him the benefit of the doubt, let him know how tactless his comments are. With luck he'll be a bit more sensitive in the future, but if this doesn't make any difference, at least you'll have a clear picture of how little he considers your feelings.

He hurts me, but I still love him

From time to time my boyfriend loses his temper and lashes out at me. Usually it's only a slap or a shake, but twice he's left bruises on my arms and body that I've had to hide from my parents and friends. I know he can't help it because he's so sorry afterwards that he even cries. He says it's because he was badly treated as a child. I love him so much that I want to understand and help him, but my best friend suspects that he hurts me and says I must leave him at once. What can I do for the best?

I'm with your friend on this. Your boyfriend has a problem, which may well have something to do with his abusive childhood. But I'm far more worried by the fact that he is now abusing you – and that you are cooperating by forgiving him and allowing him to do it again. I appreciate that he's beside himself with sorrow immediately afterwards, but that is exactly how a violent or abusive person excuses his actions to himself and manages to gain sympathy from his victim. And you are a victim here. No matter how you may think you are trying to help him, allowing this to continue only reinforces his deep-rooted belief that it's OK to treat girls and women like this. And you also stand the risk of growing to believe that this is how you should be treated. Many women who have an early abusive relationship go on to 'fall in love' with other men who treat them the same way.

You both need help. Talk to your mum and ring one of the helplines in the Contacts section for confidential and down-to-earth advice. Then, with their support, tell your boyfriend you aren't prepared to go on like this. He needs help too, but you can't force him to get it and you are not in a position to give it. However, by making the break, you might help him realise that his problem is out of hand.

I can't cope with his jealousy

I've been in a steady relationship with my boyfriend for nearly six months and everything would be perfect if it wasn't for his jealousy and moodiness. My friends keep complaining that I never see them anymore, but whenever I try to make an arrangement he goes into a sulk and says I'm neglecting him. I feel so guilty because I know that he loves me to bits and would do absolutely anything for me. Normally I talk to my mum about this, but ever since she found out that we are sleeping together she has disapproved of him. He seems to spend his whole time worrying that I'll leave him and go off with someone else. We row about it all the time, so how can

I get him to understand that I really do love him?

For someone in love you seem to be having a very hard time of it. You miss your friends and feel bad when you can't see them. Things are difficult with your mum and you're rowing with your boyfriend a lot. It's not exactly a picture of perfect bliss!

Your boyfriend is insecure and jealous. That's a real problem, but it isn't one that you can cure. He will go on making demands from you and you will continue to try to prove your love, but you will never satisfy his nagging insecurities. Jealousy is less about loving another person than an attempt to fill a bottomless hole in your own self-confidence. It is destructive and it ruins relationships. Rather than trying to prove your love, you need to place the responsibility for all this firmly back in his hands. He can get advice and help for his problem from a telephone helpline or, even better, a face-to-face youth counselling service (see Contacts for details). You might also want to talk to someone about how all this is affecting *you*. In the meantime make a real effort to build bridges with your mum and your friends. They love you and want to help you, so don't cut them out of your life.

Boys Talk!

How would you feel if you discovered your girlfriend had got off with someone else?

Sad, angry, let down.
Cortez, 17

Annoyed, angry, betrayed.
Anon

Hurt, but I'd think it was good it happened sooner rather than later.
Daniel, 16

Really upset and hurt. It would depend on how long we'd been together.
Max, 16

Hurt, sad and possibly violent towards the bloke.
Tim, 17

I'd want to kill the bastard.
Bruno, 17

I'd want revenge; I'd get off with all her friends.
Charles, 17

I'd feel unbelievably sick and disappointed.
Tom, 16

I'd be angry, but I'd try to stay calm, so she could explain what had happened.
Phil, 16

When it happened to me I rang her up and told her I didn't want to speak to her anymore, then left her in the dark for ages and never spoke to her again.
Robbie, 17

I'd go off on one. I'm not a violent person, but I'd beat him up quite a bit and I'd have serious talks with my girlfriend.
Henry, 17

Very upset and I'd feel like I'd failed. I'd lose trust in her.
Rob, 17

Disappointed and worried I wasn't good enough.
James, 16

Gutted! Mad! Stupid! Humiliated!
Jay, 17

Would it mean the end of the relationship?

Yes.
Jack, 17

Not necessarily, but it could be.
Damian, 17

Depends on the factors, like alcohol or a fight we'd just had.
Daniel, 16

Probably, unless there were good reasons and she didn't like him anything like as much as me.
David, 17

Depends on how long we were together and the circumstance of the kiss.
Tim, 17

Potentially, depending on how drunk she was.
Nick, 16

Only if I was sure it meant she really didn't feel anything for me anymore.
Anon

I don't believe he's really finished with her

My boyfriend went on holiday with some of his friends and met another girl. I wouldn't have known about it if his friends hadn't started dropping hints, and then I found a card from her in his pocket. I was so upset, and the fact that he'd lied to me by saying that he'd been faithful while the others were out with girls just made it worse. He tells me it doesn't mean anything and that it's all over, but I find it very hard to trust him. Whenever I don't know where he is, I worry he's seeing someone else. I can't stop myself asking him or ringing him up and I know it's causing a problem.

He has probably already tried to make endless excuses for his behaviour! They were away on their own, his friends were all doing it and, most of all, he didn't think it would ever affect you because you'd never find out.

But you did and it's caused a big problem.

However, if you continue to put pressure on him all the time, then you will split up, because neither of you will be able to stand it. Whether or not he repeats his adventure is totally under his control. He knows how much it hurt you, but beyond that, there's nothing more you can say to affect his behaviour. If you really feel you could never trust him again, then it might be better to finish with him now. But if you decide to stay, even though what happened wasn't your fault, you will have to make an effort to control your suspicion and jealousy. It's understandable that, given what happened, you feel the need to know where he is and what he's doing, but love isn't about possession and control. You also have to be able to trust, and trusting always involves risk. You won't be able to change how you feel overnight, but take it one day at a time. Make a pact with yourself that, for a whole twenty-four hours, you are not going to ask him where he is or what he's doing. Once you've managed this for a few days, you'll feel a great relief because checking on him all the time is stressful for you too. It might help to ask a friend or your mum to support you in this so you have someone sympathetic to talk to when the temptation gets too great.

We got carried away, and now I regret it

We've been together for five months and he's my first serious boyfriend. He knows that I don't feel ready to have sex yet. However, we went to a party and had a lot to drink. He came back with me because my parents were out, and we ended up having sex. He didn't force me or anything and, at the time, I wanted to. But afterwards I felt terrible. I was so scared I'd get pregnant and so relieved when my period started the next week. Now he can't understand why I won't do it again and I'm scared it's going to break us up.

Society makes such a fuss about virginity that it's easy to assume that once you've lost it, it doesn't matter what you do. That really isn't so! Sex can be a wonderful experience and the excitement that goes with it can be overpowering. You've felt it yourself, though the alcohol also fuelled your passion. However, sex should be about love, trust and sharing. You regret what happened, but you also take responsibility for it. You've decided that you don't want to do it again – at least for the moment. If your boyfriend respects you, then he should understand that as well. Otherwise he's using emotional blackmail to force you into something you don't want. You can talk this over in private with a helpline or with a counsellor at one of the special young people's clinics, like Brook (see Contacts). They can also give you information and advice about birth control, including pregnancy testing and emergency contraception, plus the risks and signs of STIs

91

(sexually transmitted infections). Most of all, they'll be able to reassure you of your right to make up your own mind and wait until you are ready.

Should I tell his parents the truth?

My boyfriend lied to his parents about my age by telling them I was older than I am. Sometimes I stay overnight at his house, but my mum thinks we sleep in separate rooms. When he stays at our house he sleeps on the sofa bed. I'm not exactly deceiving anyone, but I still feel uncomfortable.

The longer this goes on, the more uncomfortable you'll feel. Your boyfriend lied to get what he wanted and, even though that was his choice, you are having to cope with the results of that lie. If you are under sixteen (seventeen in Northern Ireland), then he could also be breaking the law. You must tell him how bad you feel. If you have any sort of future together, his parents will find out your age sooner or later. Better he tells them now than it causing big problems in the future.

If, as I assume from your letter, you are having sex with him, then you need to be aware of the risks and make sure you have proper protection organised. That means reading up on it and talking to your doctor or a young people's health clinic (see Contacts for more information). Presumably your mother is also worried about this and that's why you're nervous about her knowing the truth. Whether or not you tell her is up to you, but you should at least be able to give her honest reassurance that you will be careful and get advice when you need it.

Should I tell my boyfriend I have bulimia?

I suffer from bulimia, but my boyfriend of two years doesn't know. I don't know what to do. If I tell him I'm afraid he'll leave me or not understand, but I can't continue without him knowing.

Bulimia, like most eating disorders, is often linked to low self-confidence and self-esteem. Worrying about your boyfriend finding out will only make you and your problem worse, so confiding in him is definitely the right decision. Tell him you have a problem that you want to share with him. Explain that bulimia is an illness that you've been battling with for some time and you feel bad for not letting him know earlier. He may ask questions about it. It's up to you how much you want to disclose, but you could find talking really helps. It's possible he will feel a bit hurt or annoyed that you have kept this secret for so long, so explain that you were scared of what he would think and you are telling him now because you don't want any secrets between you. If you're already getting support for your eating disorder, tell your boyfriend, so he understands what's happening. If you aren't getting help yet, then hopefully bringing it out into the open will encourage you to do so. If either of you wants more information you can contact the Eating Disorders Association or look at their excellent website (see the Contacts section).

I'm scared my boyfriend will hurt himself

I'm very worried about my boyfriend. I know he's having a hard time at home at the moment, but he's become very withdrawn and moody. Sometimes he really frightens me by saying that life's not worth living or that the world will be better off without him. I've told him how much this scares me, but he says I don't understand.

Depression is a major problem in young men and, while young people of both sexes do attempt suicide, boys are more likely to succeed. If he's having problems at home then it's possible that you are closer to him at the moment than anyone else. You know there's something wrong and you know he needs help. This is a very difficult position for you, but the best thing you can do is encourage him to talk and, in particular, to contact a helpline or an adult that he trusts to discuss how he's feeling. See Contacts for suggestions.

You could offer to be with him while he did this, or to sit in the next room, for moral support. He may not like the idea, but it's important you tell him how worried you are and how much you want him to get help. If he refuses or feels unable to do it, then you must talk to someone yourself. You can't handle this responsibility on your own. Tell an adult – either your mum or one of the teachers you trust at school. You can also call one of the helplines for confidential support and advice.

Chapter 5

Taking Things Further

I'm scared he'll tell everyone I can't kiss

I go to an all-girls school and my friends talk about boys constantly. Rather than admit that I've never had a boyfriend, I've let them think that I have been out with boys and done stuff. Now I have met someone and we've been going out together for three weeks. Whenever he tries to kiss me I pull away because I'm scared of getting it wrong. To make matters worse, he's a brother of one of my friends and I'm scared they'll all find out that I don't know how to kiss.

I bet both he and your friends are a lot less experienced than they make out and are all secretly just as nervous as you.

Many people are worried about kissing for the first time, but there really is no right or wrong way to do it. Even an experienced kisser is likely to bump noses and clunk teeth with a new partner and learning to adjust to each other's style is all part of falling in love. However, just because he's asked you out doesn't necessarily mean he's right for you. Be choosy and don't stick your tongue in someone's mouth just because you think you ought to.

If you do want to try kissing, let him make the first move. As he moves in, let your mouth go soft so your lips move as he moves his mouth on yours. This is the point where there's always a bit of readjustment to get your noses in the right position. The most sensitive part of your mouth is on the outside of your lips and just where they meet. Feel your lips gently with a finger and you'll see what I mean. Moving your pressed mouths together stimulates this area and feels very good – with the right person!

I wear a brace – will it put boys off?

I've been asked out, but I wear a fitted brace and I'm scared it will put him off. What if we started to kiss and it made him feel sick or something?

He's asked you out because he likes you. And, unless he's blind, he already knows you wear a brace. Lots of girls (and boys) worry about kissing in this situation, but all the feedback I've ever received has been totally positive. If the chemistry's right between the two of you, a bit of mouth furniture won't make a difference.

I don't feel comfortable doing more than kissing

I've kissed several boys, but it never lasts for very long. They always want to take things further and I don't feel very comfortable with that. Yet most of my friends make out they've either had sex or been fingered. If this is true, does it make me a freak?

Peer pressure has a lot to answer for here. Because sex is seen as something mature and sophisticated (not always true, by the way!), some young people like to make out they're more experienced than they really are. And once one or two people start boasting, others will be tempted to exaggerate their level of experience so as not to feel left out.

The legal age for sex is sixteen (seventeen in Northern Ireland), although surveys suggest that between a quarter and a third of young people have their first sexual experience before this age. This still means that the majority don't have sex until sixteen or much later – so you certainly aren't alone. And it would definitely be wrong to try anything as intimate as sex unless you really trusted and felt comfortable with the other person.

Surveys of young people have also revealed another interesting point. When asked at what age they think their friends first started having sex, most young people believe their peer group started before them. In other words it's common to think that everyone's doing something you're not. But this pressure can lead you into doing something for which you aren't ready.

Sex at the right time and with the right person can be wonderful and amazing. Doing it just to keep up with your friends' fantasy lives is only ever going to end in disappointment and pain.

Boys Talk!

If you were going out with a girl you really liked, but she said she wasn't ready for a sexual relationship, how would you feel and what would you do?

Accept it.
Henry, 17

Respect her wishes.
James, 16

I wouldn't really mind. In fact, I'd respect her.
Tom, 16

I wouldn't mind. We'd just go on as normal.
Aron, 17

You should wait for them if it's a worthwhile relationship.
Anon

It wouldn't bother me.
Steve, 16

If I liked her that much I'd continue going out with her.
Chas, 17

I'd respect her decision and wait until she was ready.
Nick, 16

I wouldn't mind that much and if I liked her I'd definitely continue with the relationship.
Phil, 16

He thinks it's time we had sex

I've been going out with my boyfriend for nearly six months and, although I really love him, I'm not sure I'm ready to take things further yet. His parents are going away on holiday and he's staying at home on his own. He wants me to stay over and for us to make love. I don't know how to tell him I'm not ready and I'm scared I'll lose him if I do.

You can't blame him for trying! Here is what must seem an amazing opportunity – an empty house, giving you somewhere safe and comfortable to make love. He's probably been thinking about it for a long time and his friends may also be pushing him to take the opportunity. But he isn't alone in this decision. You have feelings and you have to tell him what they are. Just look him in the eye and explain that you understand how convenient and great it would be, but, in spite of all that, you don't feel ready to have sex yet – with anyone. If he loves you and cares for you he'll put his disappointment to one side and respect your decision.

If all he wants is to be able to boast to his friends that he's slept with you, then yes, there is a chance you might lose him. But, if that's the case, you'd be better off without him anyway.

Of course, that still leaves the problem of what you do do while his house is empty. I'm sure you're aware there are many ways to become more intimate and loving without going all the way and having intercourse. The problem is that touching and stroking and hugging (and getting naked together) are all very arousing and it's extremely easy to get carried away. That's why talking about how you feel and what you want is so important. Set limits now so that you both understand how far you're prepared to go. You can always renegotiate or change these later, but it's much better if your first experience of sex is something planned and looked forward to, rather than the result of getting carried away in the heat of the moment.

He won't take no for an answer

My boyfriend is desperate for us to sleep together. I've told him that I want to wait, but he says he loves me so there's no point in waiting. I'm scared that if I don't give in to him, he'll go and find someone else and that would break my heart. What should I do?

This is classic emotional blackmail. If he honestly cared for you, he would be prepared to understand your feelings and wait. If you're scared he'll leave you for someone else, it suggests he's far more interested in sex than in you and your relationship. Forever is a long time, but if he is in this for the foreseeable future, waiting a bit longer won't do any harm.

You might find it useful to talk this through with a counsellor at a young peoples' clinic, like Brook (see the Contacts section for details). They'll help you look at the situation clearly to make sure that any decision you make is yours and not the result of emotional pressure or blackmail.

Why won't he do anything more than kiss?

I really like my boyfriend, but unlike other guys, he doesn't seem to be sex-mad. We kiss and hug, but I'd like to take things further. Whenever I try to suggest it, he makes an excuse or changes the subject. I've asked him whether he wants to break up and he says no. I can't understand it. What can I do?

Boys have feelings too! And, just like girls, they all develop at different rates and have different attitudes towards love and relationships. Maybe he doesn't feel ready for this sort of commitment yet. If so, that's a good sign – it would mean he saw sex and your relationship as something serious. Maybe he has religious or cultural beliefs which make it taboo. Or perhaps he's nervous about his own performance. Just like girls, boys can become very frightened about doing things right, and putting pressure on him will only increase his anxiety.

Talk to him, but rather than making it a make-or-break 'Do you want to stay with me or not?' conversation, try to explore his thoughts on how he sees things developing between you.

Boys Talk!

Do you think that boys ever go out with a girl just because they're hoping she will have sex with them? If so, how do you feel about this?

Yep. It's up to the girl to be wise to it.
Henry, 17

Definitely. It's sad that girls are being used for their bodies. I reckon most boys are immature.
Chris, 16

Yes, but girls can always say no if they don't want to do it.
Anon

Yeah, but only real losers – not me. It's not really right and that's why I wouldn't do it.
Tom, 16

Yes. It's not right, but it definitely happens.
Phil, 16

Some might – probably too many!
Aron, 17

Oh yes. I do it.
Dan, 18

Yes, but in my opinion it's not right.
Steve, 16

Yes, but if a girl doesn't have a problem with it then it doesn't matter.
Ben, 17

He keeps comparing me to his ex

I'm fifteen and I'm going out with a boy four years older. We do quite a lot, but he makes it clear he wants to go all the way. He keeps on talking about how he used to sleep with his ex-girlfriend and how great it was. I've told him I think he's only after one thing, but he says no, he loves me.

Whether he loves you or not, he's putting you under pressure. You know you don't want to have sex yet, so he's making you feel very uncomfortable. At nineteen, he would also be breaking the law by doing anything sexual with you because you are under the age of consent. You should know that some men particularly enjoy the excitement of trying to seduce younger girls. It's a kind of power trip and has little to do with what you want or feel.

You must ask him to back off. If he does love you he'll understand and will also stop saying such insensitive things about his ex. If, on the other hand, he really is only after one thing, that will soon become obvious and you will have a much clearer idea of where you stand. It's always hard to end a relationship, but if it isn't doing you any good, it's less painful to be out than in.

I'm scared he'll think I'm too young

My boyfriend is much older than me and has a job and a car. I met him at a party and I couldn't believe he'd be interested. He took my number and called me the next day. My parents have met him and are worried about the age difference, but he's been really nice to my mum, giving her flowers and stuff, and saying he'll look after me. Boys my own age wouldn't bother to do that and it seems to have done the trick. My problem is that we spend most of our time with his friends who all drink and smoke and are heavily into clubbing. I feel a bit uncomfortable because I'm not like that and sometimes he makes comments about me being a baby because I won't join in. I'm worried he'll decide I am too young and dump me. What can I do?

He knows how old you are and he went to the trouble of buttering up your mum so he could see you. But now you're feeling under pressure to drink and do stuff that doesn't feel right. The only way forward is to tell him how you feel. If he really wants to change you into somebody else, then there's not much point in staying together. Hopefully, when he understands how things seem from your perspective, he'll reassure you and back off a bit. Maybe you could suggest doing some stuff on your own or spending some time with your friends for a change.

A word of warning, however. What do you know about his relationship history? Has he had other younger girlfriends before? If so, it might suggest he enjoys the chase and the thrill of getting them into heavier stuff. Men who do this then drop them because the novelty wears off. It's understandable to feel nervous and excited going out with someone new and older, but if you also feel uncomfortable and under pressure, then it's a warning sign that the relationship might not be doing you any good. If you are in any doubt, talk it through with a trusted friend, a counsellor or a helpline (see the Contacts section).

I'm scared he'll try to touch me again

I've been with my boyfriend about six weeks and I thought we'd both agreed that we were too young to start having sex. A week ago we went to a party together and both had quite a bit to drink. We were in one of the bedrooms kissing, and suddenly he pushed me down and put his hands up my skirt and top. At first I didn't do anything because I was really shocked, and then I told him to stop. But it seemed like ages before he did. We went home and although we've seen each other since, neither of us have mentioned it. I don't want to get him into trouble, but I'm scared of being on my own with him now, although I don't want to lose him. What should I do?

Alcohol, like any other drug, works by altering your mood and lowering your defences. Drinking makes you more likely to do something you wouldn't normally do. In his case, he tried to force you into a sexual situation, and you very nearly allowed it to happen. Drunk or not, by forcing himself upon you, he was breaking your trust and, in legal terms, this was assault.

I think you'd be better off without someone who treats you like this, but if you are going to stay together, you must talk about it. He's probably ashamed and embarrassed and may hope that you don't remember anything. He needs to know how upset you are and to understand you would never let him do anything like that again. Even so, if you still feel frightened of being with him, you must break away.

It would help to talk to a counsellor or helpline about this. See the contacts section for suggestions. Discussing it in confidence with a sensitive and trained advisor will help you work out your feelings towards your boyfriend and rehearse what you're going to say to him.

I'm starting to wish I hadn't said no

There's a boy I've liked for a long time and recently at a party we got off and it felt great. Then things went further and he asked me to sleep with him. I was really drunk and very tempted, but, mainly because I'm a virgin, I said no. Since then he's hardly spoken to me. I still like him a lot and keep thinking that I blew my chance. I want to explain how I feel, but I don't know how to do it. I've given him my phone number and suggested he call me, but he hasn't. How can I get back to how we were?

Sorry, you're looking for a happy ending here and I can't give you one. It's a very common story. You are attracted to each other and eventually the spark ignites. But, because the flame is only fuelled by lust and there's no deeper relationship, as soon as you refuse to do what he wants, he walks away. I know you dream of putting the clock back and playing it differently, but it wouldn't make any difference. If he was really interested in you and not just sex, he'd take the trouble to get to know you. But he hasn't, has he?

Don't blame yourself. This is his problem, not yours. Try to console yourself with the knowledge that if you had slept with him, he'd probably have dropped you soon afterwards anyway. Luckily, not all boys are like this, so don't waste your time grieving over this one.

Boys Talk!

If someone your age was going to have sex with a regular girlfriend, how long would they expect to go out with the girl before starting a sexual relationship?

Six months.
Anon

Three weeks minimum – but then again, I still go out with girls who I know won't do it!
Henry, 17

Two months, but it depends how old you are. If you're fifteen it's different to if you're seventeen or if it's your first relationship.
Chris, 16

A month seems reasonable – but maybe I'm just being hopeful!
Tom, 16

At least a month.
Phil, 16

A couple of months probably.
Aron, 17

Three to four months.
Nick, 16

At least a month.
Dan, 18

He doesn't know I'm a virgin

It looks as if my boyfriend and I will be having sex quite soon. I'm pleased about this, but also nervous. When we first met I knew he had had a couple of serious relationships before and I let him think I was more experienced than I am. I haven't exactly lied, but he doesn't know that I am still a virgin. Will he be able to tell when we make love?

Slow down a minute! Are you sure you're ready for this and aren't just doing it because you think he expects it? Sex is about trust and sharing, so you ought to be able to feel comfortable telling him the truth. Apart from anything else, being a girl's first partner is a tremendous privilege and it also has responsibilities. First-time sex can be uncomfortable or even painful and he needs to know so he can take things gently and slowly. You may also bleed a little after making love for the first time and, if this happens, he is bound to suspect. Apart from that, though, he won't know unless you tell him. It's the fact that you don't feel able to do that which worries me so much.

If you love and trust him, then be honest. If you can't, perhaps this isn't the right time or the right boy for you.

How can you tell when you're ready to have sex?

Although I've had boyfriends before, I've never slept with them, even though I knew some of my friends were doing it. But with this boy I feel different and there's something really special going on between us. Now I'm wondering whether we should take things further, but I don't know how you tell whether it's the right thing to do.

There's no easy answer to this, but ruling out some of the wrong reasons to have sex could help make the picture clearer.

Ask yourself whether you're doing it because you're scared of losing him or because you think everyone else is having sex. Or is it because you've been together a while, kissed and touched and done lots of other things and sex seems the obvious next step? Or are you just taking advantage of an opportunity – maybe you have an empty house or you're going on holiday together.

But if these are not the reasons and you think you are ready, it's important to know that having sex can change things dramatically – especially for girls. Apart from the risk of pregnancy and sexually transmitted infections, sleeping with someone makes you very emotionally vulnerable. That's why it's so important you really trust your partner.

Having sex for the first time when you're drunk or on drugs is a particularly bad idea. You're less likely to use proper protection and far more likely to regret it afterwards. You should also know that first-time sex, just like first-time kissing, is often clumsy and uncoordinated. It's only when two people have the opportunity to practise lovemaking together and really share their feelings and emotions that they develop the skills and experience which make for good sex. So there's not much point in starting something you don't foresee being able to continue safely and comfortably.

The key to good sex is the thing that's so important in any relationship – communication. Talk to your boyfriend about this and explore your feelings together. Be honest about what worries you and listen to what he thinks as well. Be prepared. Find out as much as you can about the risks and sensible precautions. Talk to your doctor, family planning clinic or a specialist young peoples' centre (see the Contacts section for more information). Your boyfriend can go with you if you like. Finding out about contraception and safer sex doesn't commit you to having sex, but it is useful in working out how you really feel and helps make sure you're safe when the time does come.

I'm embarrassed to ask him about contraception

We've decided we really want to sleep together and I know it's going to happen soon. The thing is, we haven't said anything about contraception yet. I think my boyfriend knows what he's doing because it's not his first time. But I'm too embarrassed to ask him if he's sure or what we will use.

If you're too embarrassed to talk about contraception (and therefore take responsibility for what you're going to do) then you're not ready to have sex. It's as simple as that. This is your body and your health you're playing with. Assuming he knows what he's doing is far too big a gamble. Get in touch with your local family planning clinic or young people's clinic and find out about contraception and safer sex – for example, condoms are the only type of birth control that also gives protection from STIs (sexually transmitted infections). The fpa (family planning association) does great leaflets; see the Contacts section for how to get hold of them. The Brook website can also answer many of your questions, but you still need to talk about all this with your boyfriend and then get further advice if necessary.

Will my parents find out I've been to a clinic?

We've been together for six months and have decided we're ready to take things further. It will be the first time for both of us and we want to make sure it's safe, so I've decided to go on the Pill. I'm going to go to the local clinic and my boyfriend has offered to come with me. I'm worried that they might contact my parents or our family doctor who might mention it to my mum. Are clinics confidential?

Even if you're under the age of consent – sixteen (seventeen in Northern Ireland) – you are still entitled to confidential advice about sexual health and free contraception if the doctor you see judges you are able to understand what you're being told and make appropriate decisions. In practice, this means that any young person who is sensible enough to go and ask a professional doctor or counsellor for help will be given the information and support they need. It is the doctor's and the clinic's duty to keep this confidential and, while they may encourage you to talk to your parents yourselves, they will not give out any information without your consent.

When visiting a clinic you will be asked about your family medical history. This is important because there are some conditions which could make using some types of contraception, like the Pill, dangerous for you. Luckily there are many different sorts of contraception available, although only condoms (male or female) protect from STIs as well. For more information, contact Brook or Sexwise (see Contacts). The clinic will also ask for details of your family doctor, but it's up to you whether or not you give these and even if you do, you can still ask that they are not informed that you are receiving contraception. However, it's in your best interests to let your doctor know, because there may come a time when you need medicines or treatment from your family doctor that will interfere with the contraception you're taking. Your family GP, like any other doctor, has to keep all this private and confidential.

Do go and talk to the clinic. They will be able to answer all your questions and reassure you.

Should I tell my mother we're sleeping together?

My boyfriend and I have decided to have sex and I'm going on the Pill. My mum knows and likes him, and has always said that I can ask her anything, but I've felt too embarrassed to discuss this with her. I wonder, though, if I should be telling her, but I can't imagine how I'd say it.

I'm sure it will already have crossed your mother's mind that things could be getting serious. By encouraging you to ask her for advice, she has tried to leave the lines of communication open, but I do appreciate how difficult it is to break this kind of news. Plus, of course, you feel this is private and something very special to the two of you.

However, because your mother will worry (that's what mothers do), perhaps you should drop a hint in a roundabout way, by telling her that you've been speaking to a doctor or clinic about contraception. This doesn't necessarily mean that you're having sex now or are even about to do so in the immediate future, but it will reassure her that you're acting responsibly and taking sensible precautions.

By the way, even if you do take the Pill, it's still a good idea to use condoms as well. Known as the 'double Dutch method', the Pill and condoms together give you double protection in case one type of contraception should fail. And unlike the Pill, condoms also protect both of you from sexually transmitted infections.

Where can I get the Morning After Pill?

We've had sex several times and we usually use a condom, but we got carried away and did it without one.

Now I'm really scared and I don't want to have to wait and see whether my next period appears in order to know whether I'm pregnant. Where can I get the Morning After Pill so that I can make sure everything's all right now?

The Morning After Pill – more correctly called emergency contraception – is usually two doses of hormones, which can be taken up to seventy-two hours (three days) after unprotected sex. The earlier you take it, the better chance of success it has. If you're over sixteen you can buy emergency contraception from most pharmacies, but girls and women of any age can get it free from their family doctor, a family planning clinic, a special sexual advice clinic, like Brook, or a hospital Accident and Emergency department. If you are going to get it from your own doctor or a clinic, you should either go in person or ring for an appointment and tell the receptionist that it is for emergency contraception. That way you should be seen the same day. If you are too late for this, wait until your next period is due and do a pregnancy test – either at home with one bought from a chemist's or supermarket, or at a clinic. If you are pregnant, it is vital you talk to a counsellor as soon as possible to consider your options. And remember that unprotected sex also leaves you at risk of STIs (sexually transmitted infections). Have a look at the Brook website (see Contacts) for more information.

Chapter 6

Breaking Up

I don't know where I stand

My boyfriend never makes any effort. It's always me who rings him or goes round to his place, but even when I do, it's like he can hardly be bothered to talk to me. One of his best mates told me at school that I'd been dumped, but when I asked my boyfriend if it was true he said he wasn't sure. Should I dump him? I don't want to lose him, but I'm really miserable.

Not only is this relationship completely one-sided, it's also very hard to see what you get out of it. Yes, you have the privilege of saying you've got a boyfriend, but he doesn't actually act like one in any way, does he? You're scared of losing him, but being with him doesn't give you any fun or pleasure either. You might find being single more fun. For your own protection you need to make a break. Tell him that you can't see any point in going on together, and then keep out of his way. He's either hoping you'll take the initiative and break up with him, or is genuinely confused and unsure of what he wants. If he's really bored, then splitting up, while painful, is going to happen whatever you do. But if he's just bewildered and confused, not seeing you for a while may help him to concentrate so he realises just how important you are to him.

I don't want to hurt his feelings

There's a boy at school who's been nagging me for ages to go out with him. I don't fancy him at all, but I do feel sorry for him so I eventually said yes. I knew right away that it wouldn't work and we've been going out now for two weeks and everyone thinks we're a couple. I don't want to hurt his feelings because he's really sweet. But I don't know what to do.

It must have taken him a lot of courage to carry on asking you out when you clearly weren't that keen, so he deserves to be let down gently. But you do still have to do it! There's no need to twist the knife by saying you don't fancy him. Explaining that you've realised you're not ready for anything heavy would be much kinder.

If possible, do it in person, either face-to-face or over the phone. Emphasise how much you like him and point out that you don't want to hurt him by pretending things are OK when they aren't. It won't be easy and he'll probably keep on asking you why. You will need to stand firm and tell him that even if he can't understand how you feel, it's still over.

How can I tell him it's over?

I was friends with my boyfriend for years before we started going out and, to tell the truth, I was much happier that way. I really like him and love him as a friend, but I just feel embarrassed and creepy when he kisses me. He doesn't realise and keeps ringing me up and asking me out and I find myself making excuses not to see him. We used to be able to talk about anything, but now when I'm alone with him I just feel awkward because I know he wants to get off with me. I'd never do anything to hurt him, but I can't go on like this.

You are going to have to face up to the fact that there's no way you're both going to be happy here! As things stand, you're miserable every time the phone rings or he gets you on your own. He probably feels wretched because you're always 'busy' or making excuses to avoid him. At least if you split up he'll have a chance to meet someone else and, with time, you might be able to go back to being just good friends. Looking at things this way you will see it is cruel to lead him on and let him think the two of you have a future together. So give both of you a break!

Be at least partially honest and explain how much you miss his friendship and that you regret the way things changed when you started going out. Say you need some breathing space and ask if it would be possible to go back to being friends for a while so you can sort out your feelings. This lets him down gently, even though the truth is you're very unlikely to get back together.

I keep cheating on my boyfriend

I broke up with my ex because I liked another boy, but now I realise he doesn't measure up to what I had before. My ex still isn't speaking to me, but in the last couple of months I've got off with two other boys at parties, even though I'm still supposed to be with my new boyfriend. I know it can't go on like this and all my friends say I have to tell him, but I just don't know how to. Should I ask them to do it for me?

You're being a wimp and you know it! You're messing around behind his back in the hope that he'll catch on and dump you just so you don't have to sort out the situation yourself. This is the sort of behaviour that girls often complain about in boys! OK, so your ex doesn't seem interested in you at the moment, but that isn't an excuse to make someone else's life a misery. What you're doing is unfair as well as cowardly, and you have to tell your new boyfriend. Using a friend as a go-between will only make it worse. You got yourself into this, now you have to find the courage to get yourself out.

Boys Talk!

What's the worst break-up you've ever had – or could imagine having?

Being dumped in public.
Leify, 16

Her telling me out loud in front of my friends.
Stretch, 17

If she cheated on me.
Joe, 15

Breaking up with me for someone else without telling me the whole truth. Even if it's hard to take, I'd at least like to know there was someone else instead of constantly wondering why.
Nick, 16

When I found out through friends (after she finished with me) that she had cheated on me on holiday.
Dustin, 16

I slept with someone else. My girlfriend was very depressed and tried to commit suicide.
Tim, 17

She got off with my best friend, so I lost them both.
Dan, 18

If a girl just disappeared with some other guy while I was away, it would make me feel so inadequate, and it would be hard to trust anyone again.
Tom, 16

I broke up with her and went back again three times, but things only got worse, not better.
Henry, 17

Normally when I'm dumped, I'm too upset to speak to the girl. This has resulted in losing a good friendship in the past. Once it even meant that I found myself unable to speak to her friends when she was around, so it wasn't just one friend I lost.
Rob, 17

I once dumped a girlfriend by text. I think she still hates me!
James, 16

The worst was when my ex and I started throwing the most evil insults possible. We really hurt each other.
Anon

Ending on bad terms because we'd started as such good friends.
Daniel, 16

Breaking up because you walked in on your girlfriend with another bloke.
Jay, 17

I can't accept that it's over

I had a holiday job during the summer and met the most amazing boy. He is three years older than me and when we started going out together, his mates gave him a hard time. Eventually, even though he said he really cared for me, he dumped me. Now I'm back at school and I can't bear not seeing him. All my friends are dating people of their own age and I feel so lonely. When we broke up we both said we could still be friends, so I've been writing him letters and ringing and texting him. But he's stopped taking my calls and he never returns my texts. I miss him so much and I just want him to know how much I love him.

Accepting that something is over can be hard – and painful. He has obviously tried to let you down gently and has said all the right things about still being friends. But he's also made it clear that there is no future for the two of you as a couple. If there was any doubt about this, his lack of response to your calls and texts certainly proves it. But you are so caught up in the misery of loving and missing him you seem unable to see this. Every time you write or text him that little flicker of hope flares up inside you managing to persuade you that somehow, some way, this time it could work. But it isn't working, and it won't.

I know this is the last thing you want to hear, but someone has to tell you straight. You are becoming obsessed with this boy and if you continue your letters and calls, he could become extremely angry. You have to learn to let go. It isn't easy, particularly when all your friends seem so happy, but you must turn to one of them or your mum for support. Ask them to help you resist the temptation to get in touch with him. Whenever you feel the urge, ring and talk to them instead. You won't feel better overnight, but stopping this behaviour will give your broken heart a chance to heal. (There's also the very slight possibility that, when he stops hearing from you, he could actually begin to miss you. Just don't hold your breath!)

He won't leave me alone

I went out with a boy for a few weeks, but ended it because I never felt comfortable with him. Now he won't leave me alone. I've had to ask my mum to answer the phone at home and make excuses for me, but I'm even thinking of changing my mobile number because he's started calling me from different phones so I don't always know it's him. He waits for me outside school or suddenly jumps out at me while I'm walking home. I've even seen him hanging about outside our house late at night. I don't think he's dangerous, but sometimes it really scares me anyway. I don't know what to do.

Just like the girl in the letter above, this boy is finding it impossible to let go. In his heart he is convinced that you love him and, no matter what you do or say, it won't make any difference. This is affecting your life and it isn't doing him much good either. He isn't going to end it so you have to put a stop to it. I'm glad you've already told your mum about the phone calls. Now it's time to tell her the whole story, so that she can understand how upset you are. Then, either you or your parents need to tell him very clearly that, unless he stops bothering you, you're going to take serious action. Your phone provider can give you advice on dealing with nuisance calls and, if he continues to stalk you or follow you home, you should get in touch with the police. Hopefully he isn't a danger, but a quiet chat from a friendly neighbourhood policeman could help him see sense.

Boys Talk!

What would cause the biggest row between you and your girlfriend?

Her finding out I was seeing someone else!
Jack, 17

Cheating by either of us.
Cortez, 17

Her taking the piss out of me.
Stretch, 17

Her not trusting me.
Daniel, 16

If I thought she was keeping big secrets about herself that involved other boys.
Jon, 17

Me wanting a more 'open' relationship – to see other people.
Nick, 16

Her getting off with another guy.
Will, 16

She accused me of being obsessive, clingy and too nice!
Henry, 17

I'm not really the argumentative type. I normally back down to avoid a row.
Rob, 17

Disloyalty to each other.
Anon

Would you be able to make up afterwards? If so, how?

Yes, any way possible.
Damian, 17

I hope so, but if we did split up I wouldn't want it to be with bad feeling. Making up would depend on what she wanted. But if I felt really unhappy I think I'd rather split up with her because in the long run it's less painful.
Nick, 16

If I caught her kissing another guy there's no way I'd make up, but I'd forgive her for minor things.
Will, 16

Yes, discuss the problem until it's sorted.
Max, 16

Cuddle, cuddle!
MacIntyre, 17

She discovered I'd slept with someone else, so that was the end of it. She wasn't a happy chappy!
Tim, 17

Yes, by being calm and reasonable.
Nick X, 17

I don't think we could make up. If she cheated I couldn't forgive her and if I were to cheat I couldn't forgive myself.
Anon

No, I'm stubborn and can't forgive and forget.
Bob, 17

My girlfriend and I were both very jealous and it caused lots of rows. Eventually we realised it was stupid and we both try harder now.
Dom, 16

My friends say I'd be mad to dump him

I'm going out with a really cute boy and I know all my friends are envious. The thing is, it just isn't working out, and I never feel comfortable when I'm with him. I've decided to finish it, but all my friends think that I'm absolutely mad. They say he's crazy about me and I should give him another chance. Should I listen to them?

Who's going out with him – you or your friends? OK, so he may look cute as anything, but you're the one on the inside of the relationship and you know how you feel. If it isn't right for you, then you should finish it. It's not fair on either of you to pretend otherwise.

At least it will put him back on the open market and one of your friends might get lucky! You'll probably feel strange if this happens, but at least you'll know you made the right decision.

I'm scared of being on my own

I'm seventeen and have been seeing my boyfriend for two years. I was one of the first of my friends to have a serious relationship, but now most of them have paired off. Everyone thinks we're really happy, but the truth is we're both bored. The magic's worn off and we know everything there is to know about each other. I realise we ought to finish it, but I'm scared of being on my own. All my friends are busy with their boyfriends and I couldn't bear everyone's sympathy. Also, I am very fond of my boyfriend and I wouldn't want to hurt him, even though I suspect he feels the same way as I do.

You know perfectly well that none of the reasons you give for staying together really stand up. The truth is, you'd rather put up with a flat and unexciting relationship than face having to spend a Saturday night on your own. It's definitely time you broke free.

You've been with this boy since you were fifteen, so in the last two years, you've both changed a lot. It's not coincidence that most teenage relationships break up within a year or two. The rate of emotional change at this time in your life is too fast and unpredictable to be able to bank on someone else following exactly the same path. There's no shame in admitting that you've grown apart and, if what you suspect is true, saying it out loud will be a relief to both of you.

Being on your own will feel scary and you'll have to make more effort about arranging things to do and meeting up with friends. But, given that relationships break up all the time, you won't be the only one of your friends in this situation for long. And until you start going out and doing things you're not likely to begin meeting other boys. Breaking up is a bridge you have to cross before you can get on with the rest of your life. The bridge may be wobbly, but there's an adventure waiting on the other side.

He says he can't live without me

I told my boyfriend that it's over, but he just won't accept it. He gets really upset and keeps ringing me up, telling me how bad he feels. I know it's all my fault and I'm really scared he'll do something stupid. He keeps asking me to give him another chance or at least to get back together until after our exams. What can I do?

You have to stand firm. You had your reasons for deciding that it was over and, presumably, those still hold true. He is using the age-old technique of emotional blackmail, and you're falling for it. You're worried about him and you're starting to feel guilty and responsible. Don't! He has problems, but he needs to find a way to solve them on his own. Tell him you're worried, but suggest he gets counselling or calls a helpline. See the Contacts section at the back of the book for some suggestions.

Don't even think of getting back together 'just until exams are over'. When that day comes, he'll most likely have another excuse and another date to try to hold you to.

If you're really scared for him, tell your parents or a teacher at school, or even talk to his mum. Help him get help, but don't give in to his threats.

Boys Talk!

If your girlfriend wanted to end the relationship, what is the kindest way she could let you know?

By telling me straight and to the point.
David, 17

Telling me that she's got problems and needs some time.
Stretch, 17

By telling the truth. Even if it's not nice to hear you can at least respect her for being honest.
Joe, 15

Quietly, personally and in confidence.
Daniel, 16

Telling me herself, face-to-face.
Jon, 17

By talking it through with me. The truth is the least painful way in the long run.
Nick, 16

I'd want her to tell me quietly and calmly with respect for my feelings.
MacKenzie, 16

I'd like her to introduce me to one of her most attractive friends
Charles, 17

Don't drop it like an H-bomb. Make me feel wanted,
but just not right for her.
Anon

There is no kind way.
James, 16

I don't want to split up until I find someone else

*I feel really mean saying this, but I know my relationship
with my boyfriend is coming to an end. However, mainly
because I don't want to be the only one without a
boyfriend, I'm reluctant to do anything about it until I
meet someone else. I don't exactly want to go behind his
back, I just need to know that someone else wants me
before I make the move. Is this very wrong?*

I admire your honesty! It's definitely unfair and ultimately
damaging to both of you – but it's also very
understandable. You don't want to abandon your current
relationship until you can find someone else to cling to.
The trouble is, when you're desperate, it's tempting to see
any passing boy as a potential life raft and easy to end
up in a relationship that's unsuitable or even damaging.
You have to set yourself free before you can think of
moving on. If you don't believe me, imagine some boy
coming up to you and saying, 'I really like you, but I'm

not prepared to dump my girlfriend until I'm sure you are right for me.' How would you feel?

It's hard seeing my ex with a new girlfriend

It was my choice to split up six months ago and I'm now very happy with a new boy as well as still being reasonably good friends with my ex. Why, then, is it so difficult for me to see my ex with his new girlfriend? I know I don't want him back, but I felt sick when I first saw them together. Does it mean I've made the wrong decision?

Presumably you had your reasons for splitting up when you did and, if everything is fine in your new relationship, you don't regret that now. The problem is that although you have moved on, in your mind, your ex is still exactly the same as he was when you left him. In other words, you expect him either to be in love with you or pining because you've dumped him. Seeing him happy and entwined with somebody else is a bit of a shock and is bound to raise a little bit of jealousy in your heart. If you can be mature enough to admit this to yourself, you're halfway to overcoming the problem.

I got dumped because I was too young

I'm fifteen and started going out with an eighteen-year-old boy I met on my Saturday job. Even though I've got other older friends, he seemed different and I really liked him. But everything was always complicated and he'd often change his mind about meeting me at the last minute, though always with some excuse. One evening he arranged to meet me in town after school, but he was an hour late turning up. When he did come, he walked straight past me and over to where some of his mates were standing on the other side of the square. I walked away and thought he'd come after me, but he didn't. The next day I saw one of his mates, who told me I'd been dumped. When I asked why, he said it was because they'd all been laughing about how young I was. I want to tell my boyfriend that he shouldn't listen to his mates and that the age difference doesn't matter, but I'm scared he won't talk to me.

Maybe his friends really were making fun of him because of the age gap and perhaps he genuinely is a sensitive and caring young man who was so worried about hurting your feelings that he let one of those friends tell you you'd been dumped. And pigs might fly!

He messed you around, then stood you up and couldn't even be bothered to make one of his feeble excuses. This is certainly about an age gap, but he's the one who's immature. He isn't worth your time or energy. I know you're hurt, but it's nothing compared with how hurt you'd be if you carried on seeing him. Ring up some friends, have a girls' night in, and get him out of your system. And next time some boy starts treating you as disrespectfully as this, make sure you're the one who does the dumping first.

I shouldn't have told him I loved him

I fell in love with my boyfriend the first time I saw him. I asked him out several times, but he kept saying no. Then, just as I was about to give up hope, we got off with each other at a party and started going out. He was everything I ever wanted and when we'd been together a month, I told him how much I loved him and how right we were for each other. He went very quiet and the next day he rang up and said he thought we should cool things off. I can't bear it. I'm so unhappy that I can't eat or sleep. Everyone says I should just forget him and that I'll meet someone else, but I can't.

You set your heart on him and built him up to be the centre of your life and now, of course, you're devastated when he walks away. Sadly, however strongly you like or love someone, you can't make them feel the same way. I know that the depth of emotion inside you must seem like enough for two, but it doesn't work that way.

Yes, you did scare him off when you told him you loved him, but he was honest enough to be able to back away rather than take advantage of your adoration.

You have to accept it's over, and you're going to need time to grieve. Maybe you weren't together for very long, but in your mind, he'd taken on immense significance and you'd pinned your hopes of happiness on him. You will get over this, but in the meantime, it would help to talk about it. Have a good cry on your best mate's shoulder, but try to talk to your mum or another adult about it too. The Samaritans (see Contacts) are always ready to listen as well.

I can't see any future without him

I broke up with my boyfriend three months ago and I feel I can't live without him. I didn't see it coming and it was a complete shock. He said he wanted us to finish. He told me there wasn't anybody else, but I now know he's with another girl. I feel shattered and I've lost all my confidence. How could he feel like that when everything seemed so right? I can't believe I'll ever be able to trust anyone again and I doubt any other boy will ever look at me. I don't want to go out and I've fallen out with my best friend because of this. I just feel that my life is over.

Breaking up, particularly when it wasn't your decision, is hell. I don't know how long you were together, but you've invested so much love and emotion in this relationship that your self-image and self-confidence have started to lean on the fact that he loved you. So, when he told you he was leaving, everything you believed about yourself seemed to crumble away. You miss him desperately, but you're also grieving for your own sense of self. You're not sure who you are anymore and all you can feel is the pain of your loss.

Nothing will take the feeling of loss away, but you can help yourself by trying to look at the situation from a different perspective. At the moment, you're focusing on the 'fact' that because he left you, you can't be worth loving. The truth is, he did love you for a while, but then things changed and he left the relationship. That doesn't mean you aren't amazing, loveable and totally desirable to someone else. And you don't have to be half of a partnership in order to feel whole.

One of the secrets of survival in any relationship is for each person to keep their own strong sense of identity. Joining together in love is wonderful, but if you lose sight of who you really are, you risk not only your happiness but also the survival of the relationship.

I know you're depressed and going out seems too much trouble, but you must make an effort. Get in touch with your best friend and explain you've been feeling lousy, but suggest you get together – soon. You don't have to start dating again yet. Just try picking up the phone and reaching out to friends and family. Make sure you've got a shoulder to cry on. Lean on your mum or use a helpline or counsellor. Fight for your happiness. You don't have to lie down and accept that life is over.

Boys Talk!

How could you or your girlfriend make breaking up less painful?

Make sure you stay friends.
David, 17

By being comforting.
Cortez, 17

By keeping it quiet and not making it something that everyone else knows about.
Stretch, 17

Try to be less emotional – it makes it much easier.
Anon

By doing it mutually and discussing the break-up. Of course, this only works if you both feel the same way!
Daniel, 16

Be honest and talk to each other rather than finding out from someone else.
Jon, 17

Do it quickly.
MacIntyre, 17

It's easier if you try not to get too emotionally attached too quickly.
Tim, 17

Do it gradually – take a break first, then if it's OK,

split up. If you both regret it, you can try again.
Tom, 16

It makes it easier if you hate each other. Just sever all ties.
N, 17

Don't try to see each other again. Getting back together for old times' sake doesn't work.
Henry, 17 (who split up and went back to his girlfriend three times)

It's harder at the time, but doing it face-to-face usually makes it better in the long run.
Rob, 17

Try to use tact. Don't be blunt, and make sure you say something nice as well as the inevitable.
Ivor, 16

It's just not possible to have an easy break-up.
James, 16

I can't stop thinking about my ex

Even though I saw it coming, it was still a shock when we broke up a month ago. Everyone is being really kind to me, but I can't get him out of my mind. Everything I see and hear reminds me of him and I spend every night sitting in my room thinking about it and crying. I know I need to move on, but how can I when he fills my thoughts like this?

When a relationship is over – for whatever reason – you grieve for what you have lost. And, just like the grief that follows a death, you are tossed around in a storm of different emotions. You may feel angry, lost, lonely, confused, guilty and despairing. Accepting that these emotions are going to occupy you for a while is healthy, but it's still an exhausting process!

Sometimes making your own ritual to help put an end to these obsessive thoughts can be very useful. It won't make you forget about him altogether, but it may help build a bridge for you to step from the past into the future. Set yourself a date and resolve that at that point you'll have one last major grief-fest where you'll go over all the old memories and then you'll lock it all away and be ready to move on. Ask a trusted friend to help you. Gather up all the photos, mementos, funny cards and love notes. Sit down, go through it all and weep for what is past. Then either destroy at least part of it or put it all into a box and seal it up with lots and lots of sticky tape. Put it away at the back of a wardrobe, turn your back on it and tell yourself that you're free. It would help if you could immediately go out and do something with your friends, but even the knowledge that you've looked your loss in the face and survived will be a relief.

I keep pretending we are still together

I think I'm going mad because I can't seem to come to terms with the fact that we've broken up. I know he's gone, but I keep pretending he's just away on holiday or something. I hadn't realised how much I was fooling myself until someone mentioned him the other day and asked me if I knew him. I immediately said yes, he's my boyfriend. But he isn't and hasn't been for months. Am I going crazy?

You're in denial. Your mind is trying to protect you from the pain of splitting up by telling itself little white lies. The fact that you're beginning to be aware of what's going on suggests that you're ready to face up to reality and accept the inevitable. Using a ritual like the one just described in the previous answer, or inventing one for yourself may help. It might also be a good idea to talk to a counsellor and get some support for the next few weeks.

He said we could still be friends, but now he won't talk to me

My boyfriend and I had quite a rocky relationship. Early on he got off with another girl and I suppose I always found it difficult to trust him after that. Later I started seeing an old boyfriend on the side, and when he found out, he was furious. We split up, but I apologised and we got back together again for two months until he finished with me for good. We both knew that it wasn't going to last at this point, so we agreed we could still be friends. I phoned him a few times and we arranged to meet up for a drink just as friends, but he didn't turn up. He apologised and said he still wanted to be friends and that he'd phone me in a couple of days, but he hasn't. I know it's over, but I find it very hard to let go and I don't want to lose him altogether.

Although women are often thought to be the more passionate of the sexes, research suggests that men do find it harder to forgive and forget. When one partner has an affair in a marriage, statistics show that wives are more likely to forgive a husband's infidelity and allow the marriage to continue. When the situation is reversed, the men usually insist on divorce. This may be a matter of masculine pride or a difference between male and female brains, as some men can find it harder to work around things and negotiate. Either way, it causes tremendous problems between the sexes.

You can't force your ex to do something he isn't ready for. He's angry and confused and, even if he does still want to be in touch with you, he may not be able to do it at the moment.

Give him time. Stay out of contact because, hard as it seems, it will reduce the pain and increase the chance of him deciding that he does miss you after all.

Chapter 7

Moving On

Why do I keep going back to him?

I have a very on-off relationship with a boy. I never mean to go back to him, but somehow he always finds the right thing to say, even though he's cheated on me twice. I know this isn't doing me any good, but how do I stop myself from falling for him again?

It would help if you could work out what it is that pulls you back each time. Do you have the misguided notion that somehow you'll be able to change his behaviour simply by loving him enough? If so, forget it. He is the one in control here, and anyway, however much you love someone, you can't force them to feel something they don't.

Maybe you crave the excitement? Each time you kiss and make up, you feel all thrilled and hopeful. Then he lets you down again and you're left disappointed and alone. It's easy to become addicted to these highs (and lows) and to believe that love should always be a roller-coaster of emotions.

Or maybe on subconscious level you think you deserve this type of treatment? The victims of abusive behaviour often come to believe that they're only getting what is due to them.

The bottom line is, if you do go back to him, you will only be hurt again. People do sometimes change, but it's a lot more common for them to carry on acting as they've done before. You know how painful that is, so you have to make the decision to stay away. Talking this through with someone can help, particularly if you can ring them or lean on them the next time he tries to tempt you back.

I want to be friends with my ex, but we end up arguing all the time

I went out with my ex for fourteen months, but things just started to get too heavy and complicated and I broke it off last year. It wasn't easy and I'm still very fond of him, but I know it was the right thing to do. The problem is, we said we'd be friends and we still see each other a lot because we have the same friends, but we always end up rowing. I know he wants me back and that's why he's often nasty to me. But, although I do miss him, I couldn't get back with him because I'd just be messing him around. What can I do?

This relationship has been over for months now, but neither of you has really let go. The only answer is to give each other some space. That can be difficult when you mix with the same crowd, but you have to work at it. If he's still harbouring hopes that the two of you will get back together, then every time he sees you, he'll try to raise the emotional temperature. You resent this, he gets frustrated and the next thing you know, you're having a row.

There's no way that the two of you can be just friends until you've both had time to cool off. If you can't avoid him altogether, make sure you're never alone with him. And if he gets in a state or starts trying to provoke an argument, just turn away and leave him to it. By all means tell him you're doing it for his own good, but make sure you keep on doing it!

My ex keeps criticising me and it's making me miserable

I went out with my ex for six months, but we split up earlier this year. Ever since then he's made a point of badmouthing anything I do, all my friends and, in particular, any boy I show an interest in. He makes out it's because he's worried about me, but it's really irritating and often upsets me a lot. He also goes on about all the other girls he likes. Is he doing it just to make me jealous?

You bet he is! I don't know who decided on the initial break-up, but he certainly is taking pleasure in winding you up and adding a sour note to everything you do. The only way to prevent that is to make sure he doesn't get the chance. He's obviously good with words and knows how to hit you in your tender spots, so tell him you've had enough of his badmouthing and 'concern' for your well-being, then walk away before he can reply.

Keep out of his way for a while – or make sure you only see him when there are other, more understanding, friends around. Once he understands that his words no longer hurt you, he will stop acting like this.

I'm scared of my ex even though I still love him

I broke up with my boyfriend because of his violent temper and jealousy. Several times he hurt me so much that I had to hide it from my parents. I was so ashamed that I couldn't tell anyone, but even so I still loved him. Finally I found out something bad about him and he really lost it. He said that if I ever told anyone he'd kill me. And I believe him.

Now he's spreading lies and rumours about me and last week he got me on my own and threatened me again. I don't know what to do.

This boy is immature, spiteful and very likely dangerous. Even though it was so hard, you did the right thing in leaving him and you must resist any temptation to go back to try to make things better.

Unfortunately he's still got a hold on you through his bullying and rumour-mongering. It's really important that you confide in someone, preferably an adult. He needs to be stopped for his own sake as well as yours. Please talk to your mum, but I also want you to call ChildLine or the NSPCC helpline (see Contacts). They can advise you further and help you work through your feelings and fears.

I want to get back with my ex, but he won't finish with his new girlfriend

I went out with a boy for three months and was absolutely crazy about him. It ended when I got drunk at a party and got off with someone else. I couldn't believe what I'd done and was totally miserable. Soon after that he started going out with another girl I know vaguely. I tried not to let my feelings show, but I couldn't bear seeing them together. Then, two weeks ago, we got talking and he said we'd still be together if I hadn't got drunk at that party. The next thing I knew we were kissing and hugging, and I thought everything was going to be all right. But he's still with the other girl. I've seen him twice since then and always get off with him, but it doesn't seem to make any difference. Should I wait for him or find someone else?

Look, maybe I'm being stupid, but I don't quite get the concept of 'waiting' for him. To put it bluntly, you're there sitting on a plate whenever he wants you. He doesn't even have to pretend that he isn't running back to his full-time girlfriend afterwards. He's stringing you along and doing exactly what he wants, without offering you the slightest hope of a more serious relationship.

You have two choices. Carry on like this and you'll end up with a bad reputation and he'll still go back to someone else all the time. Or tell him you're not prepared to put up with this and that he knows where to find you if he's ever interested in treating you properly. He may not come running, but at least you'll survive with your dignity and reputation intact.

Can a long-distance relationship work?

I met my boyfriend two years ago on holiday and ever since then we've been writing, phoning and emailing each other. We've only managed to meet three times since, but we both know that we're in love and I've told him that I'll wait for as long as it takes. However, my friends all make fun of me and say I should get out and see other boys, and even my mum is trying to persuade me to ease things off a bit. I really want this to work, but is there any chance that it will?

Long-distance relationships conducted by email and phone can be incredibly intense, but there's also a risk that they're an excuse to escape from real life.

If the bond between the two of you is really strong, then it will survive the distance and maybe even a few outside relationships. But if you never put it to the test and stay locked inside your room emailing twenty-four hours a day, you'll never really know whether what you have is real or just a cyberspace fantasy that will turn to dust in the daylight.

Because you write and speak to each other so much, you may be more emotionally intimate than other couples who see each other every night, but words on their own aren't enough. Until you're with someone in person for a long period of time you can't really tell how the chemistry will work.

I'm inclined to think you should listen to your mum and your friends. It's important to keep your own life going, and that may mean at least mixing with and talking to other boys.

He wants us to go to the same university

We're filling in our UCAS forms and I've chosen a uni with a course that I really want to do. I thought my boyfriend wanted to go somewhere else, but now he's decided to apply to the same place as me. I'm flattered, but I also feel crowded. I do love him, but I'm looking forward to going off to uni and, although I'd miss him if he wasn't there, I'm worried I'll also miss out on the full experience if he's by my side all the time. What should I do?

Going away to university is an amazing experience. You'll probably feel more stimulated, excited, tired and lonely than ever before – and all within the first week! It can be very tempting to hold on to a familiar hand, but this also means you don't get the full experience. Many deep and lasting friendships are made during the first couple of terms and, if you are part of an already established couple, the chances are you'll miss out on a lot of these. If things go wrong later and you split up it can be very hard to find your feet.

If your relationship is strong enough, it will survive the stress of going to different universities. There probably will be some wobbles and doubts, but if you're meant to make it, you will. Your boyfriend's insistence on coming to the same college either sounds like an attempt to control you or a need on his part for an emotional comfort blanket. Either way it doesn't seem to be what you want. Tell him you're worried and ask him to make very sure he is choosing the best course and place for what he wants to do. If necessary, call his bluff by saying you've changed your mind and see whether he still seems to want to go to what was your choice. But, when it comes to filling in the form and making your application, you must choose what is best for *you*. If he does still insist on coming to the same place, make sure that you at least live separately to start off with so that you have a chance to make your own circle of friends.

Boys Talk!

Do you think couples who have been going out for a while should try to apply to the same university?

No, not really.
Damian, 17

No – they'd be jeopardising their education.
Joe, 15

If possible – yes. But neither one's ambitions should be jeopardised as a result of the relationship.
Cortez, 17

If they value their relationship over their education there's not much problem, but they have to consider how important that relationship is.
Nick, 16

Not necessarily – you should go to a university that's right for you and your future. If your girlfriend goes there too that's a bonus.
MacKenzie, 16

Yes, if they are in love.
Will, 16

No, go to the uni that's best for you and your course rather than where your girlfriend or boyfriend is going.
Tim, 17

If they want. If it offers good courses for both of them.
Dan, 18

If they see a future for the relationship, then definitely.
Tom, 16

Only if they see themselves spending the rest of their lives together.
Phil, 16

Depends. They could distract each other – or be great study partners.
G, 17

No, it's a co-dependence that shouldn't carry on forever!
Nick X, 17

Not really because you should apply to the university *you* want to go to.
Rob, 17

Yes, good couples should try and stay together. They would have great memories.
James, 16

No, only if they *really* want to do the same course. Uni is very different from school.
Ivor, 16

If they don't both go to the same university, should they make each other any promises?

No, never make promises.
Jack, 17

No, long-distance relationships don't work.
Stretch, 17

Yes, you should promise not to cheat on each other and see each other as often as possible.
Joe, 15

It's difficult. You could try, but you should also agree to keep an open mind. I'd want to argue that university is a chance to meet new people, so I couldn't make absolute guarantees.
Dan, 18

No, if they like each other enough they don't need to make promises.
Jon, 17

If they're going to be a long way apart, seeing new people is inevitable, so promises in these circumstances can be easily broken.
Nick, 16

I would try and tell my girlfriend I would be faithful – but 'party on, dude!'
Will, 16

It depends on whether they feel strong enough to keep those promises.
MacKenzie, 16

No, they probably won't keep them anyway. It would be very hard, but I would have to tell my girlfriend what I thought.
Phil, 16

It depends. They should obviously talk about it and see what they decide, but it seems like a perfect opportunity to meet new people, so having a break might be best.
Robbie, 17

No. If you're not actually together it would be too hard, and I wouldn't want to make a promise I couldn't keep.
James, 16

I'm scared he'll dump me when he goes to university

We started going out six months ago and have recently begun sleeping together. I know it's serious, and my boyfriend says he loves me. He's going to university in October and I'm already worried about how much I will miss him. But the thing that scares me most is that many of his friends who have been in supposedly stable relationships are now breaking up with their girlfriends. He knows I'm worried and says he doesn't intend to do the same, but admits that ultimately there can be no guarantees. I'm so upset that I now find it difficult to be with him, though I don't want to ruin the time we have left together. What should I do?

There's no denying that he will face many temptations

and pressures once he's at university, and there's no way you'll be able to hang on to him if he decides to break loose. But that's in the future. You need to find a way to live with your fear in the meantime. He's given you as much reassurance as he can. Saying that there are 'no guarantees' may seem harsh, but it's also honest. Therefore, it's likely he will tell you the truth if he does change his mind, rather than string you along while he sees other people.

As for his friends, I suspect they're using university as an excuse to finish with their girlfriends. In fact, they're probably already starting to play the field, aren't they? Your boyfriend isn't doing this. I can't make any promises for the future, but you should try to enjoy what you have while you have it.

When he does go away, you'll need to agree how to handle things. You have to accept that he'll be going out to parties and clubs, etc., and enjoying himself. If you're sitting at home waiting for him to call or email, you could feel very lonely and vulnerable. You might decide that it's better to give each other some freedom for a couple of months and agree to meet up again at Christmas and see how you both feel. This won't be an easy decision, but it will give you time to re-assess your relationship. Most of all, don't put too much pressure on him because that's the fastest route to losing him altogether.

Why do we keep rowing just as he's going away?

My boyfriend of eighteen months is going off on a gap year while I finish my A-levels. We've talked about this a lot and we know we can make no absolute promises, but we hope that we'll both still want to be together when he comes back. I'm really going to miss him, but I'm trying to be as brave and positive as possible, because I know it's hard for him too. However, as his date of departure gets closer we are rowing more and more. It's nothing serious, just lots of petty squabbles, but it's unsettling. Does it mean we should break up and get it over with?

No one else but you and your boyfriend can answer that. However, it's worth bearing in mind that when a separation is about to occur people often act in this way. The anticipation of the pain of being apart becomes too great to bear. Because of this you may both be trying (without realising it) to distance yourself from the situation by picking these petty rows. Try talking about this and accepting it for what it probably is – last minute nerves.

I want to get engaged before he leaves

My boyfriend's taking a gap year and going travelling after Christmas. I am sixteen and he's eighteen, but we're very much in love. We've talked about it and have agreed that we're going to carry on, even though we won't be able to see each other for months. However, I'm still very scared of losing him and I think we should get engaged before he goes. He's not so sure, but he says he loves me, so I don't see any reason why we shouldn't. How can I persuade him?

Slow down a minute! It's absolutely not the time to get engaged. I know that you are legally old enough, but you both have a long way to go before you can make any plans for marriage.

You want a ring on your finger, because you think it will make you feel safer. In fact, it won't make any difference at all. The more pressure you put on him, the more likely you are to lose him altogether. If you love him, you also have to trust him. And be generous enough to allow him the freedom to enjoy this adventure. If he still comes back to you, you will know that what you have is precious and true.

Contacts and Further Help

The following organisations, websites and helplines can give you and/or your boyfriend free, confidential advice and information

Note: numbers beginning '0800' or '0500' are freephone and don't show up on phone bills.

General health and medical advice

NHS Direct
24-hour free medical advice.
0845 4647
www.nhsdirect.nhs.uk

www.wiredforhealth.gov.uk
www.mindbodysoul.gov.uk
www.teenagehealthfreak.org
Lots of useful information on teenage health and growing up.

www.thesite.org.uk
Info on sex, relationships and much more for 16- to 25-year-olds.

www.menshealthforum.org.uk
www.malehealth.co.uk

Info and research on men's health.

Sexual health and advice

Sexwise

Free advice and information on sex and relationships for under 19s.

0800 28 29 30

www.ruthinking.co.uk (includes details of services throughout UK)

Brook

A network of special young people's clinics and an excellent website. They provide free, confidential sex advice and contraception for young people under 25.

0800 0185 023

www.brook.org.uk

Family planning association (FPA)

Medical advice and information on contraception, pregnancy and STIs. Helplines are open Mon–Fri.

www.fpa.org.uk

England & Wales 0845 310 1334

Scotland 0141 576 5088

Northern Ireland 02890 325488

www.likeitis.org.uk

Useful info on sex and relationships for young people.

The London Lesbian and Gay Switchboard

This website has links to regional Lesbian and Gay Switchboards in the UK, offering confidential support and information nationwide. Open 24 hours.

020 7837 7324

www.llgs.org.uk

National AIDS Helpline

Free and confidential advice on HIV and other STIs.

0800 137 437

www.aidshelpline.org.uk

Avert

An international AIDS and HIV charity. The website has an excellent section for young people with info on sex and contraception as well as HIV and STIs.

www.avert.org

For depression, difficulties with parents, relationship and emotional problems, etc.

ChildLine (UK)

24-hour free, confidential helpline for young people.

0800 1111

www.childline.org.uk

ChildLine (Ireland)

Ireland Freephone 1 800 666 666

www.there4me.com

Confidential online advice for young people, including a chance
for real-time talk with an NSPCC counsellor.

Samaritans

A 24-hour listening ear for anyone lonely, depressed or thinking of
suicide.

08457 90 90 90

www.samaritans.org.uk

Get Connected

A free helpline that can find the best service to help, whatever the
problem may be. Open 1pm–11pm daily.

0808 808 4994

www.getconnected.org.uk

Anti-Bullying Campaign

Advice for victims of bullying and their parents. Open 10am–4pm
weekdays.

020 7378 1446

www.bullying.co.uk

Who Cares? Trust

Support and advice for young people in care. Open Mon, Wed,
Thurs 3.30pm–6pm.

LinkLine 0500 564 570

www.thewhocarestrust.org.uk

The Line

ChildLine's service for young people living away from home or in care. Open weekdays 3.30pm–9.30pm, weekends 2pm–8pm.

0800 88 44 44

No Panic

Information and support for people who suffer from panic attacks, phobias and obsessive compulsive disorders (OCDs). Open 10am–10pm daily.

0808 808 0545

www.nopanic.org.uk

Saneline

Advice and support for the sufferers of mental illness and their friends and families. Open 12pm–2am daily.

0845 767 8000

www.sane.org.uk

Eating Disorders Association

Support and advice for anyone experiencing difficulties with eating. Open 4pm–8.30pm weekdays.

Youthline: 0845 634 7650

www.edauk.com

Advice and support for people struggling with addictions

Alateen

Advice if a parent or friend has problems with alcohol. Open 10am–10pm.

020 7403 0888

www.al-anon.org/alateen.html

Drinkline

Advice on alcohol problems.

Open 9am–11pm weekdays, 6pm–11pm weekends.

0800 917 8282

www.wrecked.co.uk

Quit

Free 24-hour information on how to stop smoking.

0800 002200

www.quit.org.uk

National Drugs Helpline

Open 24 hours, seven days a week.

0800 776600

www.ndh.org.uk

Advice and support for victims of abuse

ChildLine (UK)
24-hour free, confidential helpline for young people.
0800 1111
www.childline.org.uk

ChildLine (Ireland)
Ireland freephone 1800 666 666

NSPCC Helpline
Can give advice and support to any young person who has suffered or is suffering from physical, emotional or sexual abuse. (NB: This helpline does not guarantee confidentiality in cases of serious abuse, but you can ask for advice without disclosing your name or location. If in doubt, check with the helpline counsellor, who will always tell you at what point they would have to break confidentiality.
0808 800 5000
www.nspcc.org.uk

Survivors UK
Advice and support for young men who have been the victims of sexual abuse or male rape.
0845 1221201 (Tues & Thurs 7pm–10pm)
www.survivorsuk.org.uk

Legal advice for young people

Children's Legal Centre

Open 10am–12.30pm and 2pm–4.30 pm weekdays.

01206 873820

www.childrenslegalcentre.com

Index

If you would like more information about
books available from Piccadilly Press and how
to order them, please contact us at:

Piccadilly Press Ltd.
5 Castle Road
London
NW1 8PR

Tel: 020 7267 4492
Fax: 020 7267 4493

Feel free to visit our website at
www.piccadillypress.co.uk

The Story of Black History

Roy Kerridge

The Claridge Press

First published in Great Britain in 1998

by The Claridge Press
33 Canonbury Park South
London
N1 2 JW

Copyright © Roy Kerridge

Printed by
Antony Rowe Ltd
Chippenham

CIP data for this title is available from the British Library

ISBN 1-870626-22-2

Kerridge, Roy, *The Story of Black History*

1. History

For John Michell, First Hippie in Notting Hill

Author's note

In Part Nine of this book, the names Sister Dorothy, Yvonne, Anna and Shirley are not the real names of the persons involved.

Acknowledgements

I must thank the following individuals for all heir help: Julian Allen, Katie Kerridge, Michael Wharton, the late Mr Chisholm, Forgive E. Tettey, Saint Sarfo Kantanka, Razak Adio, Samuel Owusu Korranteng, Isaac Nana Asare, Patience Dansu, Evelyn Adjani, Kingsley Yensu, Prince Benjamin Amoah, Boakye Agyemang Charles and Thomas Agyemang Obvious.

Contents

Foreword

This book, "The Story of Black History", came into being as a result of a chance remark. An old family friend, "Uncle Mick" (otherwise known as Michael Ivens, poet and director of "Aims of Industry") had recently moved to Willesden.

"Willesden Green, your nearest public library, is a nest of 'Black Triumphalism'" I told him.

"What do you mean?" he asked.

"I'll write it down", I said, but my writing grew and grew and became a book.

White readers, I am told, will scarcely credit the fact that black people can believe any of the varieties of Black History examined in this book. Many black readers, however, take all such theories for granted, and will probably be amazed to learn that anyone can doubt them. Did not a professional black man, Paul Boateng, M.P. for Brent South, exclaim on winning his seat: "Four hundred years! We have been waiting four hundred years for this moment!"

If anyone had pointed out that black people had not lived in Brent for four hundred years, but for scarcely forty, he would probably have regarded such a person as mad. Hundreds of 'black intellectuals' would have put the figure at two thousand years, a long wait indeed for the Hon Member.

Such beliefs encompass both defiance ("we blacks have been left out of White History books") and a heart rending yearning for a secure place in English life (" we are not immigrants, we have been here all along"). Great Divisions, made great only by belief in their greatness, continue to plague English life. Once there was the Protestant-Catholic division, a matter of life and death in its day. Class replaced Religion as the next Great Division that men may die for, and now Race has replaced Class. When Race has run its course, so to speak, ideas such as Black History and White History may vanish, and we may rediscover English history regardless of our colour.

Part One. What is Black History?

"Black History", together with "Black Studies", is a popular college course in Britain and America today. The word "Black" in both cases means "African" or "pertaining to people of African descent." I shall now try and unravel a few of the strands of "Black History" that form such a tangled ball of yarns today.

In many parts of Africa, human history, for centuries, could be called "Black History", as few non-Negro races were present to help to make it. However, in North and South America, the Caribbean and in Britain, many races combined to make things happen. How can the "Black" be picked out of national histories and be made into a special history of its own? Are "Blacks" an international people, as Jews were once, with no nation of their own, but with a single "Black History"?

"Black History", as a separate subject, seems to have begun in "Blackademe" the newly-created college world of Black America, USA. Since its birth, thirty or forty years ago, it has spawned an Empire of academic job creation expanding alongside White Academe and often rivalling it in dottiness.

Like all Americans, the inhabitants of Blackademe assume that everyone is American, and therefore all black people are Black Americans. They write American history from a "black viewpoint", picking out black people from the rest, and concentrating on them. If questioned, they can point to books entitled "American History" and claim, quite justly, that these are books of "White History" that ignore the achievements of black people in America.

So far, so good, but when "Black History" is transposed to Britain, difficulties at once occur. Whereas the history of post-Red Indian America is a tale of black and white complexion, the history of the British Isles is mainly a story of white peoples until the close of the Second World War. American History, as popularly understood, is very short, whereas English history usually begins, in old-fashioned schoolbooks, with the landing of Julius Caesar in pre-Christian days. Such a timespan gives little scope to the truthful Black Historian, but plenty to another kind. Nowadays, the British Black Historian cannot point to a schoolbook of White History, since history in state schools has shrunk into disconnected "Information Packs" on disparate eras, and is no longer properly understood by most teachers or pupils. Ashamed of the "imperial and Christian past", which they feel to have been wholly evil, the English have quietly dropped their history.

Island Story, the title of one of my nineteen fifties school history books, would now be assumed by most scholars to be a history of Jamaica. (There is a parallel between the two small islands that sent adventurers all over the world, to seek their own fortunes and change the destinies of those whom they encountered.) However, a history of Jamaica may be well worth reading, but a book entitled "Our History" should be handled with care. "Our History", "Our People" and "Us" are words now understood in educational circles to mean either "black people" or "not to be read by white people". "Black histories" and "White histories" by their natures sacrifice truth to racial pride.

Outside the embryo British Blackademe (patron saint: Stuart Hall), West Indians and the white English are growing more friendly with one another. Our Blackademe ignores this, and apes America, refusing to accept a world-view where black and white people can share a stage. Everything is seen in black or white.

Is "history" a *true* story, or a series of national and racial myths designed to "make people feel good about themselves"? Musing on Black History and Black Studies, I fell into a Brown Study, from which I emerged to categorise concepts of British Black History. I discovered four main varieties.

1.   Windrush History, in which the ship "Empire Windrush" occupies the place held by the ship "Mayflower" in White American history. In 1948, the "Empire Windrush" brought the first large batch of hopeful mainly Jamaican West Indian immigrants to Britain.

2.   Black Presence History, in which the existence of a few black people in Britain at any given time, from the Roman Conquest to the "Empire Windrush" cut-off-date, is milked for all it is worth. "Black Presence History" has overtones of a conspiracy theory, since some of its followers believe that a large important Black Presence in England has been concealed by deceitful white historians. The arrival of West Indians in Britain on the "Empire Windrush", according to this view, brought the Concealed Black Presence into the open for the first time.

3.   Nubianism, or Eddie Murphism. This view of Black History puts Africa first, as the home of all black people. It has a strong appeal to Black Britons, as it allows them to feel African, or to feel what they *think* is African. It is actually an imported Black American dream of Africa as a Promised Land with Heavenly overtones, now reinforced by the Eddie Murphy film *Coming to America*. This film depicts an imaginary African kingdom of dreamlike splendour. Followers of this semi-religious view of history in England imagine themselves to be Black Americans pretending to be Africans.

4.   The true history (as far as can be discovered) of black people in Britain and the world, which takes in elements from the three preceding views. Yes, very many black people came to Britain from Jamaica in the late'forties, the 'fifties and the early nineteen sixties. Yet plenty of Africans and non-Caribbean black

people came here too, in a variety of ways, and adapted to Britain in a markedly non-Windrushian fashion. That is, they did not seek work in hospitals or transport. As for Black Presence History — yes, some black people have lived at docksides during the past centuries, particularly in the eighteenth century, but most white people never saw them. Nor did they greatly influence national events. Nubianism is not wholly a fantasy, since all historians acknowledge that great kingdoms and dynasties have existed in Africa from the earliest human times to the present. However, in real life these kingdoms and their people were not wholly good, or angelic, but consisted of normal fallible human beings, no better or worse than those of Europe. Subjects of African kings no more thought of themselves as "Africans" or "Blacks" than their medieval counterparts in Europe thought of themselves as "Europeans" or "Whites". A neo-Nubian can be distinguished from a "real" African by the fact that he or she will wear robes adorned somewhere with a map of the African continent.

Part Two. The Need for Black History.

Why is there such a demand for Black History? The motives and the veracity of some Black Historians can be called to question, but the yearnings of the Black British for a place in their own country form a reproach to the unpatriotic White British.

"Why am I here? Where do I belong? Who are my people?" are questions that Black History seeks to answer. Black Britons, the children of immigrants, ask these questions. Many of them, as toddlers, have repeatedly been asked "Where are you from?" by well-meaning white adults.

"England", or "London" or perhaps "Wembley" they reply.

"No, where are you *really* from?"

As the familiar Inquisition continues, the interrogator finally receives a satisfying answer: "My parents came from Jamaica/ Trinidad/Sierra Leone/Nigeria."

"I see! So you're a second generation immigrant! Never forget your roots!"

Countless reminders, kindly or unkindly meant, tell the Black British child that he or she is in the "wrong country". For many years, Black Britons sought to overcome such obstacles by being as English as possible and making English history their own. "Sought" is perhaps too strong a word, since the process seemed a natural one, the child being surrounded by "Englishness" from birth.

At some time in the late 'sixties, when most black children in London had black playmates, this anguished "integration" came to an end. I call it "anguished", and I put "integration" in inverted commas, because a young person who felt completely English would often be regarded by white friends as completely foreign. It is common to find large families where the older brothers and sisters have English accents and the younger ones have Jamaican accents. I know one large family from Trinidad where only the youngest daughter is Jamaican — a kind of sub-American sub-Jamaican-ness having become the British style of being Black. In another family, the older brother and sister move and speak in such an English way that those who know them well regard them as English. However, the *younger* sisters move, speak, sing and dance in a Black style that owes something to America and the Caribbean, but little to their father's home in West Africa.

There has been a cut-off time for the Black English. Those born before (say) 1969 may regard themselves as English but are regarded by others as Black. Those born *after* 1969 regard themselves as Black, are regarded as such by everyone else, and so should perhaps feel satisfied. But they miss having a History, and grope towards one or another of the forms of Black History I describe.

Perhaps my supposed watershed year of 1969 is significant for white people also. Those who reached maturity in that year, and the years following, are the generations who either rejected English history or never learned it in the first place. Possibly "history" began to be seen as a "black thing", of no concern to white people. When a white youth threatens someone, he often shouts "You're history, pal!" or "This time tomorrow, you'll be history!"

Instead of meaning "Your deeds and name will never die, they'll go down in history", the brawling hooligan seems to mean "You're as good as dead!" or "You'll soon be utterly forgotten."

History, to the white English, appears to mean "oblivion". Some white English people re-invent themselves as make-believe Americans, their "Mayflower" that arch-Americaniser Elvis Presley in his 'fifties heyday. Since many Black English regard themselves as Black Americans, the two ideas dovetail.

Most young white people are unaware that unpleasant Cockneys once shouted "Go back to your own country!" at black people. The new generation of black people help to make England look more American.

Most Africans and West Indians that I meet show an unusual interest in history, and love hearing about Romans, Celts, Saxons and olden-day people of every kind and every land. An African or a West Indian of the immigrant generation, born into the British Empire, usually feels loyalty towards both Britain and his or her birthplace. Loyalties of Black Britons are more complex. A youth born in England of Jamaican parents may feel loyal to Britain, to Jamaica, to an imagined paradisal Black America or to an imagined paradisal Africa. If the youth has (say) Trinidadian parents, he may feel loyal to an imagined paradisal Jamaica as well as to Trinidad. West African loyalties, Russian doll-like, contain nations, tribes and clans. To the English born, with West African parents, England, Black America, Jamaica *and* an imaginary "Nubian" Africa could be added to the list of tribes and clans. Sometimes one loyalty is firmly fixed-upon, but more often, the whole lot swirl around in a bewildering cloud of identities, each identity having its own "history".

Part Three. Windrush History

In the mid-nineteen fifties, a spate of war films was made, greatly exciting the boys at my London grammar school. Some of these films were based on autobiographical novels of the Second World War; all showed British soldiers in a fairly heroic light. For the first time, apparently, the boys understood and appreciated what had been done on their behalf, only ten, twelve or fifteen years earlier. Yet they did not see the war with their parents' eyes, but only through the deeds of the film actors. I belong to a generation that never listened to reminiscences of the war, whether these came from family, family friends or total strangers in pubs. One of the reasons why I preferred coffee bars to pubs was because in coffee bars you did not meet "some miserable old workman maundering on about the war".

Similarly, the Black English seldom listen to the true stories of sacrifice, heroism, disappointment, struggle and modest triumph that their immigrant parents could tell. Instead, seekers after Black English History see the past through television programmes, all of which show Pathé newsreels of the "Empire Windrush" bringing well-dressed optimistic Jamaicans to Tilbury, whence trains took them on to London. Much amusement is derived from the old-fashioned "Ealing comedy" accents of the newsreader, as well as from his inability to know history in advance and to realise just *what* a momentous change was taking place in English history.

Budding Black Historians often feel uneasy at the emphasis

on loyalty to the Empire evoked by the newsreels. Such loyalty was taken for granted by most of the immigrants themselves, and journalists at first urged white people to welcome their Commonwealth brethren.

"Windrush History", of course, is misleading, since thousands more Jamaicans came here on other ships and later by 'plane. The charge of "Eurocentric", sometimes levelled at white historians, makes one wonder if the word "Jamaico-centric" will ever be used against Windrush historians. So persuasive is Windrush history that two students of my acquaintance, asked to write of their family experiences on "coming to Britain", guiltily described imaginary Jamaican parents on the "Empire Windrush". In fact, both students had African fathers and English mothers.

The "Jamaico-centric" approach to history misleads many scholars, since Jamaican immigrants in the early nineteen fifties were by no means typical. Almost as many women as men disembarked from the "Windrush" and other boats coming from Jamaica. Young people steeped in Windrushiana imagine the Black London of nineteen fifty to have been a microcosm of the well-established Jamaican London of today, largely guided and dominated by determined-looking church-going women.

Reality, as I remember it, consisted of a Black London of *men*, their white English wives and girlfriends almost the only women around. Most of the men in our family circle were West Africans, a few were East African and the rest came from Trinidad. Black London was African London, and the Trinidadians soon allied themselves with Creoles from Sierra Leone, West Africa. (I should explain that my stepfather was secretary of the "African League" and editor of *The African Voice*.) The few Jamaicans we met seemed very odd fish, with their baffling allegiance to God, Queen and Commonwealth, instead of to Pan-African Unity, Russia and Stalin. None of the immigrants, Jamaican or African, envisaged for a second that a Black Britain was in the making. All expected to return back home after a while, possibly with a full purse. The *African Voice* newspaper addressed itself to the problems of Africa, not of Africans in London.

Conventional "Windrush History" is correct in implying that most newly-arrived West Indians in nineteen fifties England sought work in transport (men) or hospitals (women). My mother remembers the queues outside London Transport recruiting offices. Later, in the early 'sixties, I accompanied a Singhalese youth to one recruiting office, to find a packed waiting room, with standing room only. By that time, many of the applicants to be bus conductors were of Asiatic background. (Perhaps after standing for hours, some became conductors and then spent their time shouting "Standing Room Only" at the public.) Nowadays, Pay As You Enter buses have put an end to the glut of conductor-jobs.

According to Windrush-mythology, black people were needed to do "the jobs white people didn't want to do". If this were so, why weren't the white working class overjoyed to see them? Why didn't they cry "I'm so glad to see you — you can have my job, 'cos *I* don't want to do it"?

Instead, as I well remember, prejudiced working class people said (to one another, as they never spoke to immigrants) "They're taking our jobs!" White men between jobs (which were then easy to find) often blamed their unemployment on "black people who've got all the jobs!" Such nineteen fifties white people seemed vaguely to feel that black people were paid less than white people, but this was not the case. Trade Unionists sometimes spoke about immigrants as if they were "blacklegs" or cheap labour whose presence undervalued their own labour in some way. Ignorance about West Indians was rife, and I have often met white people who imagined the immigrants had been either slaves or "wild jungle natives" in their own countries. In the nineteen fifties, West Indians in British colonies had strong ideas about Britain, the font of all benevolence. That is why they came here, *of their own accord,* not sent for by cynical white masters, as some Black Historians believe. White people had not only *not* sent for them, but were amazed to see them, and with the best will in the world could not "place" them.

The average Englishman in nineteen fifty thought of black people as being either American Negroes or Africans. Intellectuals admired American black people for their music, songs, dances and folklore, while Christians yearned to tell Africans about Jesus. Working class people saw black people in a ribald light, as comic minstrel figures (American) or cannibal kings who boiled missionaries in cooking pots (Africans). Harry Belafonte, with his sentimentalised calypso songs, first brought West Indians to the notice of the stay-at-home English, many years after meek Jamaicans and jaunty Trinidadians had landed on these shores. (Belafonte's tuneful calypsos bear the same relation to Trinidadian calypso as Stephen Foster's plantation melodies do to the field chants of Mississippi and Louisiana.)

Misunderstood and unappreciated, the West Indians moved doggedly from one mishap to another. Africans, such as my stepfather, often fared better in dealings with white people, as Africa was a "known country" to the English. My mother has seen Jamaicans angrily shouted at by an official, for daring to ask about tax rebates to which they were entitled. In the same office, an African friend easily obtained a rebate for a wife and seven children who did not exist. Trinidadians joined the African League and declared themselves to be Africans, while less-confident Jamaicans tried in vain to join local church congregations on an equal footing. Nowadays, many Jamaicans in England have abandoned the Anglican or Methodist churches of their "back home" days, and joined Pentecostal fellowships with Caribbean pastors.

Ironically, the English-born children of West Indians often see themselves through English eyes as either American Negroes, baseball-cap variety, or as Africans of a Nubian or Ethiopian kind. Instead of listening to the true stories of their elders, they have succumbed to a misleading "Black History".

Not long ago, Hackney Museum showed an exhibition of nineteen fifties photographs of West Indians (*not* Africans) in London. Although a bit "Windrushy" in its Caribbean emphasis, the exhibit presented a truthful picture of those times, individual life stories or "case histories" printed beside the photographs. A West Indian mother and her grown-up Black British daughter wandered around the exhibition, the former deeply interested, the latter listless.

Triumphantly, the middle-aged mother paused at a photograph of an immigrant's passport.

" 'Jamaica — British West Indies' ", she read aloud with pride. "See, we were all British then!"

The daughter rolled her eyes to Heaven and said nothing. Her "Black Pride" T-shirt said it all for her.

What an indictment of Britain, that West Indians who came here as British now feel they have to belong not to a country but to a colour, not to a nation but to a race! If your race is your country, then it needs a history like every country, and so Black History was born.

As well as saying "They're taking our jobs!" a sour white workman of the nineteen fifties also might say "They're taking our women!" In my own London neighbourhood, so many white working class *and* bohemian-intellectual girls can be seen with enchanting brown children that the long-ago workman's complaint could be considered a painless *fait accompli*.

Today, "white complaint" has moved on from "They're taking our women" to "They're taking our purses." The "Windrush Historians'" view of Black Crime is one of innocent black youth being forever harried, pestered and persecuted by the police. That such persecution happens, I know only too well. But in the real-life "Windrush Years", when the dominant Negro immigrants were West Africans, the police were flummoxed by the embryo "black community" and left it alone. Apart from intellectuals, the type of white men who were most pleased to meet black people were petty criminals. Cable Street, Stepney, the post-war "black quarter", had been a vice-ridden "sailor town" for the previous hundred and fifty years. Before long, some West Africans and a few West Indians, spurned by "mainstream England", had formed a miniature Black Underworld.

This underworld, described so well by Colin MacInnes in his novel *City of Spades*, was largely ignored by the police as "nothing to do with them". If only there had been a little *more* police persecution then, the Black Britain of today might be cleansed of the taint of crime. As long as black people in London only robbed each other, and oppressed their own girlfriends, the police would turn a blind eye. If one African reported another to the police, the police would only laugh.

The Hogarthian squalor, vice and ribaldry of those early East End days is wholly unknown to the Windrushian writers of "Our History". Mother Brown, a well-known figure in early-'fifties Cable Street, was a cackling old Creole beldame from Sierra Leone, who introduced runaway girls from orphanages, Ireland and the North to African ponces in the East End. At first, the girls would be dazzled by the glamour of Cable Street. Prostitution-control, not drug peddling, was the most typical "black crime" of those days. Today, a coloured woman known as Mother Brown could safely be assumed to be a holy woman in a turban and gown, with a reputation for healing.

"Windrush Historians" sometimes give a nod to the idea that West Indians came here of their own accord by referring to the "Myth of the Motherland". But Imperial England *was* a Motherland — it was no myth. The finest produce of the Empire was sent to Britain, so why should not the people who helped to make or grow it follow on? How could free people toil with England in mind and not feel that they were involved in a wonderful enterprise as part of a wonderful country? "Can a mother's tender care — turn against the child she bear?" asks the hymn writer. Yes, it can, for not all mothers are very nice people or very clever people. It behoved the *English* to believe in the Myth of the Motherland, as of course some of them did. We all need a myth to live by, and not all myths are "mythological". Many elderly West Indians keep the Myth of the Motherland alive.

Part Four. Black Presence History.

From American "Blackademe" has come the idea that black or Negro people lived in North America before the time of Columbus. Even without this dubious bonanza of thousands of years of history unrecorded until now, Black History in America has an advantage over English Black History in that black people undeniably did live there before the nineteen fifties. As I have said earlier, there has probably been no time in the past five hundred years when there were no black people at all in England. However, one or two people here or there, living and marrying among white people, does not make a "black community". The slavery triangle in Georgian times — boats leaving Britain, laden with trade goods, sailing to Africa to buy slaves, taking the slaves to America, and carrying sugar, tobacco or cotton back to Britain — did *not* involve bringing shackled coffles of slaves to Britain. A few valets and page-boys, belonging to West India merchants, half-servants, half-slaves, could be found in Bristol and Liverpool. Slave-trading flourished as a business in enlightened Britain because the slaves were never seen by most stay-at-home Englishmen. When black slaves *were* seen in London, the captive servants of visiting West Indian planters, public outcry led to the end of slavery.

Nevertheless, "Black Presence Historians" regale us with apocryphal tales of caves in the Severn gorge filled with chained Africans, and believe fervently in a secret *continuous* "black community" purposely ignored by "White Historians". They seize on mentions of individual black people in England by the same

"White Historians" as proof of this community's existence — the Hidden Black Presence.

On television I have seen my kind-hearted Black British acquaintance Benjamin Zephaniah weeping over the grave of one "Scipio Africanus", said by the tombstone inscription to have been "born a pagan and a slave". (According to Peter Fryer, whose book *Staying Power* is often quoted and misquoted by "Black Presence Historians", Scipio became the free servant of the Earl of Suffolk and died in 1820, aged 18.)

"This shows that it's all a lie that black people came over in boats in the 'fifties to do work that white people wouldn't do!" the poet Benjamin exclaimed feelingly.

His own mother Valerie, to whom he is much attached, came to England from Jamaica in the 'fifties, no doubt with high ideals of a Motherland. Why should her story be less significant than that of poor Scipio? Evidently Scipio had been "born a slave", which is to say, he had *not been born in Britain.* One of his masters must have given him the ironic name "Scipio Africanus", first bestowed on a Roman conqueror of North Africa. "Africanus" is hardly a name one would give to a person whose ancestors had lived in England for hundreds of years. Why does Benjamin show such pride and rapture at the plight of a former slave who died a thousand miles from home, yet feel ashamed of free men and women who toiled in hospitals and factories and are now ending their days in modest prosperity?

I cannot answer for the poet Benjamin, but many of the Black Presence historians and their followers share a noble emotion, patriotism. Born in England, or brought here when very young, they love their country with all their hearts and so feel that their ancestors *must* have played a part in English History. As children, many Black English dream of days gone by, of kings, queens and valiant men and women performing great deeds beneath an English sky. They devour historical novels, and imagine themselves the heroes or heroines, with no colour-feeling at all. By the age of fifteen or so, their patriotism is often cruelly punctured by the jeers and ignorant guffaws of the white English.

One such young historian was met with amused glances at a stately home because she knew the names and the stories of the men and women whose portraits hung on the wall.

"How come *you* know all this?" somebody asked.

The same girl met with incredulity and rudeness when she tried to attend a meeting of the Sealed Knot, whose members dress up as Roundheads and Cavaliers and re-enact old battles. Sadly, the young historian turned away, tried to forget she was English and re-created herself as "a member of the black community", looking no further for the meaning of life than the message of a "rap song".

A less well-informed young person might have resolved the question differently, by a belief in an historical Black Presence, or Parallel History, in which *black* Roundheads and Cavaliers disported themselves on the English scene. Such a belief, in *black* Black Knights, black Robin Hoods dressed in Lincoln black, and so on, leads to the strangest idea of all — that white people should have moved Heaven and Earth to pretend that such black people were not there. ("I don't like you, so you're *not* history! You wait, I'll see that you're kept out of all the books!")

Black Presence Historians seem to believe that people who lived in what is now the Olden Days *knew* that they were in the Olden Days, and took care to prevent modern people from finding out about their antics. Why did they stop? Why, when the immigrants of the nineteen fifties added their numbers to a large secret Black Presence, did white people suddenly begin to record their activities? Logically, by Black Presence ideology, white people *now* should be denying that black people live in England.

I revel in English history although most of my ancestors come from Denmark and Poland. I can do so because I am white, and so am allowed to feel an affinity with the land in which I was born. Were it not for colour prejudice, there would be no Black Presence History, and my heart goes out to the sad but undefeated Black Presence believers.

Mary Seacole, a Jamaican nurse who journeyed at her own expense to the Crimean War to tend the wounded, is the patron saint of Black Presence History because she lived for a time in London. Somehow, the fact that she was born in Jamaica is glossed over, overshadowed by the greater fact that she had been left out of English History schoolbooks, while Florence Nightingale had been put in. If every person who ever lived in England, or even every person who witnessed the Fall of Sebastopol (as Mary did) were mentioned by name in all the school history books, these books would have been even longer and even more tedious than I remember them to have been. (Of course, state school history books have long been replaced by Information Packs, all brimful of Information about Mary Seacole.)

Mary Seacole and her bold exploits were chronicled in the Press of her day. However, the fact that until recently she remained a small footnote in schoolbooks has been recognised exultantly by Black Presence Historians as the Big Cover-Up, or Black Presence Concealed! Good, decent Mary Seacole has inadvertently become the one big proof of the White Falsification of History Theory. She sits uneasily beneath such laurels, for as her autobiography makes clear, she did not regard herself as a black person until she came to England. As a light-skinned "mulatto", or "clear" complexioned person in Jamaica, she belonged to the island "middle class" (just as she would do today). She referred with kindly patronage to "the black people". In London she was refused official permission to go to the Crimea, and realised with horror and with tears that to the bigwigs she too was regarded as black! Like Black English hopefuls of today, she was driven by cruelty to a form of "black consciousness", but went to the Crimea and did her duty just the same. *Punch* magazine took up her cause, and she was not unknown in the Britain of her time. A truthful historian cannot accord her the same place in history books as Florence Nightingale, who was the founder of the modern profession of nursing.

However, School Information Packs on History have now

elevated Mary Seacole to the role of English History Personi-
fied. Recently, I tried to help a twelve year old girl with her
history homework, only to be told, "What! You don't know the
date when Mary Seacole was born? I thought you said you knew
history?"

If History is seen as a Black History and a White History, at
war with one another, each continually trying to "score off" the
other side, then an unpleasant racial consciousness will poison
all our feelings. From thinking of the largely-imaginary black
people in English History as "we", the young historian is led on
to think of Black Americans as part of the same "we", since
Black History is an American concept. Black consciousness
spreads like a fungus, until all the black people of the world,
including the most disparate tribes of Africa, become "we".

"Black History" encourages the concept of "White History",
and brings into being a *white* race consciousness that transcends
national boundaries — "we white people". Fortunately, matters rarely lead up to a Logical Conclusion, for if they did, the
whole world would soon be divided into "We and They" on
battle lines of skin colour. Black people who regard all white
people as the same people can then blame not only innocent
men and women but whole nations for the crimes that quite
different white people have done.

"You people made apartheid, ran the slave trade, created
the Holocaust, dropped the bomb on Hiroshima, just because
you're white!" is the cry.

Before a fight breaks out, we shall move on to the most potentially harmful History of all. Once more, a noble idea has
been perverted to serve an evil end. I refer, of course, to....

Part Five. Eddie Murphism in America

Many of the Black English look avidly to Black America for something more than mere styles and fashion. They seek a dream world which they can re-create in England and to which they can then belong. Not only Eddie Murphy but almost all modern American Negro film actors depict worlds of black gangsterism *and* black wealth, Beverly Hills-style, from which white people are virtually excluded. Most of those who believe in a fantasy Black America are not interested in history. Children who are particularly enraptured by such American films seldom show much interest in Civil Rights struggles or the history of black people in America. Images of *poor* or enslaved peoples would jar the image of shiny black glamour which they believe exists in the here-and-now.

However, the palatial Arabian Nights-like Africa evoked in Murphy's film *Coming to America* hit a chord with history-minded adults in the USA and in England. Murphy's pill box hat, worn in the film, has become the badge of those who imagine Old Africa to have been one vast extent of parks, palaces and fountains in courtyards, with every man a King. Murphy's African Kingdom is set in the present, somewhere near the Sudan, but his followers prefer to dwell on kings and queens in bygone ages before white people appeared in Africa.

This strain of Black History had long been developed in America, but Murphy's film gave it a new impetus and popular appeal. In England, the African dreamers have become known as Nubians. They should not be confused with the inhabitants of Nubia, for the Murphy-Nubia is not of this world.

First of all, I shall take a look at the Africanists of America, since their attitudes are copied unreflectingly by the Nubians of England. If, in the year 1800, all the white people had left America for some reason, their abandoned slaves would probably have built African villages and settled down in a New Africa that might not have greatly differed from the Old. But if the white people had delayed their exit until the year 1900, a century later, the left-behind Negroes would surely have carried their "white" institutions on and perpetuated a European America. The same would happen if the white people left *now*, for the Black Man and the Red Man have become Americanised (or "Anglicised", if you prefer). This is an unpalatable fact that the Black Africanist cannot accept or stomach. Another unacceptable fact is the very existence of slavery in America. The sloughing-off of slavery occurs when a generation of Negroes arises who have been born in the North. While most American Negroes lived in the south, working for Mister So-and-So, memories of slavery were only too real. These memories persisted throughout the Flight from the South that occurred between nineteen twenty and nineteen sixty, as former sharecroppers made their homes in Chicago, Detroit, New York and the coastal cities of California. Just as some of the Black English are ashamed of their parents' old-time stories of Jamaica, so many young Black Americans *born outside the South* are ashamed of their elders' Tales of the Old Plantation. With few visible reminders of slavery around them, they have skipped two hundred years of history and are attempting to re-establish their American selves as Africans.

As they know nothing of Africa, and do not seek to find out anything that is *true* about that continent, their antics may cause others to smile. However, their desperate "African-ness" has in a sense been forced upon them by the refusal of White Americans to welcome them. So there is a pathos in "African American-ness", as there is in the similar Rastafarian cult in the West Indies.

Fashion dictates that *all* American Negroes should now be called "African Americans", but I shall use the term only to mean those black Americans who *think* of themselves as African Americans. There seems to be an uneasy seesaw of friendship and resentment between the Jewish people and the Negroes of New York. Not long ago, many American Jews thought of themselves as the friends and elder-brothers of Negroes, offering help and guidance. Jewish teachers and lawyers felt Black Power as a sharp slap on their helping hands, in the late nineteen sixties. A new Jewish generation arose who complained about black people in these terms: "My grandfather came to New York from Russia in eighteen ninety without a penny, yet in twenty years he had become a prosperous businessman. His descendants are all professional people. Black people came to America with the first settlers, hundreds of years ago, yet they *still* have nothing! Aha!"

Stung by this accusation, the black New Yorker ignores the flaw in the argument — that the Negroes were not immigrants, but slaves. An immigrant is to some extent the master of his destiny, but the slave exists at the whim of his master. One group of people came to America urging the captain of the boat "On! On! To America, Land of the Free, and away from the Old Country!" The *other* group, many years earlier, cried to the captain in vain, "Turn back! Turn back! We don't want to go! Take us home!"

The two groups of newcomers arrived in America in very different circumstances and states of mind. African Americans in modern New York have, with careful use of "Black History", created a false Black Past in which their forefathers came to American cities as immigrants straight from Africa.

The South is wiped out, the past is a clean slate upon which may be drawn images of an imaginary Africa. When real memories of "down home" are forgotten, "false memories" of Africa begin. (In Caribbean England, read "back home".) African dress and "African customs" are invented, and these, in America as in England, have become the badge of the well-to-do successful professional class of black people.

African Americans think of Africa not as a continent of many nations, but as One Country, with one language, one set of customs to be learned, and so on. Bits and pieces of customs are adapted from Islam, Judaism and so on. A complete festival, "Kwanza", has been invented by "African Americans" to take the place of Christmas. Variously described as "the Black Christmas", "the African Mid-Winter Festival" and so on, it seems to borrow from the Jewish festival of lights with more recent touches of Yoruba harvest rites. Cards wishing one (but not all) a "Happy Kwanza" are on sale in most American and English cities. Most of the cards include a message explaining "The Meaning of Kwanza" to the recipient.

Until recently, the "African Language" proclaimed by "African Americans" was Swahili, an Arab-pidgin used originally by slave traders operating from Zanzibar. The language (never learned, but often quoted) accorded well with the general "pro-Islam" slant of the New Africans. Now, after thirty years of glorifying Arabs and Islam, the neo-Africans have at last become dimly aware of the vast Arab involvement in the African slave trade. Yoruba is replacing Swahili as the "African Language", and Yoruba customs and designs are affecting New York Africana. This *may* be because many Yoruba from Nigeria have settled in New York, although on the whole neo-Africans in America and Britain resolutely ignore the existence of those people born in Africa who may live in their midst. "Real Africans" would rock the boat and disturb their dreams.

Bogus histories of Africa and Africans pour from all-American "Blackademe" to perplex the honest scholar and puff up the arrogant black Race Supremacist. A popular don at the moment is Leonard Jefferies, who has divided mankind into Ice People (bad) and Sun People (good). Ice People are white, and Sun People are black. On television, I have seen a film of Jefferies expounding his theories to a captive audience of black students who slumped despairingly before him, making notes, in the manner of students everywhere. ("I never knew Black History was so hard — I must be really silly.")

If it were ever to be admitted that not only some Arabs but many black Africans, were instrumental in the successful running of the slave trade, then Blackademe would collapse. For this reason, very little truthful history can emerge from Blackademe.

Fibs from Blackademe are no worse than the fibs of Official Television America whose quiz-and-chat-show propaganda depicts a land of "mixed marriages", one spouse Sun and the other Ice. The whole sub-continent must be scoured by talent scouts to find such couples and bring them together in a studio, an almost Russian feat of propaganda.

A prominent American Negro recently declared "I am an African who just happens to be living in America". Deportation to Africa might change his tune: "I am an American who just happens to be living in Africa. Get me home! These crazy Africans not only call me a 'foreigner', they call me a 'white man'! Plus there's only one channel on television."

It is odd to read, in unbiased history books, of the metamorphosis that came over nineteenth-century Black American leaders and "progressive thinkers", born in slavery, who emigrated to Liberia, West Africa, to start a new life. Just like Western frontiersmen, they built forts and took pot shots at the "savages." You can take the man out of America, but....

For the Africa-conscious Black American, the Negro churches and Christianity in general are an awkward reminder of slavery, of the existence of white people and of the admiration for white people felt by many black church-goers. Hence the urgent replacement of Christmas by Kwanza. African traits a-plenty can be found in unsophisticated Black Americans, who do not know that some of their ways have been handed down from slavery times and beyond. As soon as black people discover

their "African heritage", they lose their African ways.   False
Africa displaces real Africa.

On a visit to Louisiana, a state where African magic and
folklore prevails, I interviewed a musician who told me about
the Alligator Dance of her childhood, then broke off to exclaim:
"You come from England, the mother country, where our set-
tler ancestors came from!" In a church where slave-time spirituals
were sung, the black pastor greeted me joyously: "A man from
England, home of our mother-church, the great Church of England!"

Such opinions upset and embarrass the sophisticated Neo-
African, who shrinks from *real* African mannerisms. These he
regards as "low".

To return once-and-for-all to England, I have myself been
interviewed by the Rastafarian poet Benjamin Zephaniah, who
told me, in all sincerity, "I am an African who just happens to be
living in England". However, he spoke in a broad Birmingham
accent, except when he recited his Rastafarian Back-to-Africa
poetry. *Then* he spoke in a broad *Jamaican* accent. Rastafarianism,
which began as an "African Jamaican" cult, replete with invented
history, became in England a defiant badge of "authentic
Jamaicanism". So it lost its original meaning and function to
the "Nubians", the name adopted by the present generation of
pretend-Africans in Caribbean England.

Part Six. Nubianism in England.

Last week I went to a West Indian Pentecostal Church to hear a visiting American gospel singer, Twinkie Clark, who plays thumping blues piano in the style of Little Richard. A sophisticated Black American lady writer was there, who addressed the congregation as "African Caribbeans". Their lack of polish and their homely ways seemed to alarm her. However, her unease was eclipsed by the far-greater unease and appalled timidity of reporters from the English Black Press who were present.

Eagerly, the pill-box-hat African-clothed reporters and intellectuals looked to me and other white visitors as allies in an unfamiliar world. So thoroughly had they Africanised themselves, that they felt utterly cut-off from those non-intellectual Black British who had remained West Indians. Polite and quietly spoken in a most un-Jamaican style, they were far more out of place in the church than were the smart Americans and I. My heart went out to them in their plight. In another setting, they might have strutted proudly, showing their fine silken colours. They were Nubians.

From nowhere (though encouraged by *Alarm* magazine) the word "Nubian" has appeared to describe those Black Britons of Caribbean descent who refer to themselves as Africans. When feeling sure of themselves, in a Bohemian intellectual setting, they normally become very confident, cheerful and talkative. Surrounding themselves by pictures of Ancient Egyptians, they confound white admirers and enquirers with glib remarks about the superiority of "we Africans." Although Nubians give the impression of being direct descendants of Pharoahs, if not of gods, they are quite unfazed when asked awkward questions about their more recent ancestors.

"We Africans are not like you white people — we look after our old people! Where is my own mother now? Thanks to slavery and you people, she is in Barbados. But in *Africa*, as I was saying …." (Heard on a radio chat show) .

Ancient Egyptian art is the wonder of the world, so why not pay those bygone artists of genius the compliment of knowing what colour they were? If the pictures are anything to go by, an Ancient Egyptian crowd was not dissimilar in skin colour from an average bus queue in modern London — some light, some black, but nearly all brown. Nubians have created a market for pseudo-Ancient Egyptian paintings in which all the people are very black. They have a ready-made history just behind them, that of the Ancient Egyptians, with only a vague blur to cover the passing of time between Cleopatra and Eddie Murphy. With little trouble, they can open any book about Ancient Egypt and start pontificating about their ancestors. Few bother to read such books thoroughly, but on the most meagre of scraps, Nubians grow quite "drunk on words", and talk for hours without ceasing about the Land of Punt.

The mythical Land of Punt has become a King Charles's head, or obsessive topic of conversation, among Back to Africa intellectuals ever since the nineteen fifties. In modern Britain, a delinquent Americanised "black youth" often grows stout, slow and heavy in his late twenties. He then abandons petty crime, and starts living in the Land of Punt, fixing passers-by with an Ancient Mariner's eye and talking rapidly about "we Africans" and how he's now "wised up" to History.

Most Nubians have an evangelising mission to the unsaved — that is, those West Indians and Black British who do not regard themselves as Africans. "You must learn history — you must use your intellect and find out who you really are and where you're really from!" Nubians urge the unconverted. Of course, such exhortations are only addressed to black people, as in Britain it is tacitly understood by all that these are the only people who *have* a history.

However, if the person thus exhorted were to make a study of Caribbean or West African history, the Nubian would either be dumbfounded or lose his temper. Nevertheless, many Black English young men have discovered real West African history, in spite of the Black History Movement.

"My mother reckons all African gods are demons, part of the world of sin, yet I've found that some well-meaning Africans worship them quite sincerely", I once overheard a fervent young man tell his Black English friends gathered admiringly on a crowded East End railway platform. "Shango was a real man, a warrior, but he grew so famous that some Nigerians took him for a god. He's even remembered in the Caribbean today — slavery didn't take that away."

Truthful history does not please most Nubians. Slavery and West Africa are out of bounds to those who dwell in the Land of Punt, although slave-stealing white people are sometimes blamed for ending the Golden Age in Africa. Some Nubians branch out from Ancient Egypt and learn the names of kings and empires from every part of the African continent. The essence of Nubianism seems to be the creation of a dream-world, one admired and applauded by white people and respected as "educated and upper class but not for us" by ordinary West Indians and Black Britons. Disturbing truths about things that happened long ago form no part of the Nubian concept of "Black History".

Most of the olden-day African kings, emperors and indeed Pharoahs whose names are bandied about with pride by Nubians possessed slaves. During the Western slave trade, many African kings and chiefs grew rich as suppliers of slaves to Arabs and white people alike. Kings and chiefs who did *not* co-operate with outside slave traders had to fight all-comers or perish, which explains the warlike nature (or defensive nature) of many African tribes. The lightest reading of African history shows that slave trading and capturing on a large scale could never have happened without at least a modicum of African co-operation with the traders.

"Black History", from its poisoned source in American "Blackademe", constantly suppresses all such evidence. "White people", supposed to be all the same and uniformly villainous, not only invented slavery but had no part in its suppression in Africa. So we are told by Nubians and Blackademe. Wilberforce, Granville Sharpe and the whole abolitionist movement have simply been written out of history. At the best, white people supposedly "granted emancipation when slavery was no longer economically viable", but more often than not, "black people fought for and achieved their own freedom." Such ideas inculcate sneering, jeering, defiant attitudes, and bring an unhealthy mistrustful atmosphere in their wake. Many Nubians admire or pay lip service to the "Nation of Islam", an American Black Power group. Just as the Angry Brigade in the 'sixties was the militant wing of the Hippies, so the "Nation" is the severe wing of the dreamy Nubians. They now attract many young Black Englishmen. Devotees dress in penguin suits and resemble stern brainwashed Mormons.

Although the "Nation of Islam" has few links with historic Islam, relying on the Old Testament rather than the Koran as a source of inspiration, it is associated with an admiration for Arabs and a distrust of Jews. Incidentally, in view of the enormous Arab involvement in the African slave trade, it is odd that there has never been an Abolition Movement among Arabs. Philanthropic Arabs in Old Zanzibar sometimes bought hundreds of African slaves in order to set them free, but did nothing to impede the slave trade itself. Possibly they believed slavery to be endemic in Africa, and possibly they were right. Every white person who sets up home in Africa south of the Sahara is besieged by applicants for jobs as houseboys or hangers-on. By helping others, and gaining dependants, a man can become a slave-owner unawares.

Nineteenth century missionaries who freed large numbers of slaves, or gave refuge to runaways, often could not return the former slaves to their various far-flung tribes or villages. Instead, they kept them as grateful unpaid servants, or slaves if you like. In North Nigeria, missionaries established a Home for Freed Slaves, well-treated people who worked for their keep and seldom thought of running away. There is a benevolent side to slavery, *not* in Big House "Gone with the Wind" style, but small-time domestic slavery, African-style. Yet who would not rather be free than be a slave? All of the above is heresy according to Nubians and most Black Historians. The Prophet Mohammed himself might be saddened to see the faith he founded linked to slavery.

Wealthy Arabians still own black slaves, the descendants of abducted Africans, and sometimes bring them to England as servants. A Black British girl working in Harrods thus became aware of Islamic slavery, but excused it, saying that the Arab wives who came in to buy dresses were on terms of merry, giggling schoolgirlish equality with their black "maids."

"I don't call that slavery at all!" she told me, forgetting that the Arab *wives* were in a sense slaves to their almighty sheikh husbands. No wonder the wives and slave girls got on well together, for they *were* equals. Notwithstanding the benign good-fellowship, man-to-man, of most wealthy Arabs, I have yet to meet an Arabian who felt sorry about his nation's recent involvement in the slave trade. This involvement ended within living memory with the creation of British East Africa.

With the creation of the state of Israel has come about the idea that Arab and Jew are eternal opposites. When Nubians, Nation of Islam-ists, and Rastafarians become pro-Arab, they often assume that they must now become anti-Semitic. However, English Nubians are as much part of a fashion movement as of a political creed, and they excel at making beautiful robes of golden silk, together with jewelled maps of Africa as ladies' earrings and Eddie Murphy pill box hats for all, replete with imaginative "tribal designs." A lady Nubian in all her splendour is referred to as a Nubian Princess.

I have Nubian friends, graceful women and heavy young men. One of the latter sells pseudo-African knick-knacks from a peddler's tray in the entrances of Tube stations. His West Indian grandparents, who came to London in stiff Western clothes expecting to take their rightful place in British life, would be surprised to see their grandson calling himself an African and selling fake "native crafts" to white passers-by. Not that my peddler friend feels demeaned in any way — far from it. In his mind he is restoring his people to their Nubian past, a part of the forces of Progress.

Both Nubian and Nation of Islam literature make strange reading for a non-believer. Nubian meetings, held in halls during "church hours" on Sundays, are advertised by posters declaring that "Nubians are super-beings made in Africa in ancient times by immortals from space adept in arts of genetic engineering, wrongly called God."

(Nation of Islam material has been printed in America, and is taken on trust by British devotees, who surely cannot understand the American Black Power vendetta against all rural Southern customs, reminders of slavery and of realistic or truthful history. Members are strongly admonished against eating "deer, possums, coons, turtles or hominy grits", advice that seems strange when offered on the streets of Harlesden. The Nation positively fulminates against peanut butter, and if an Islam-ite saw someone eating a watermelon, he would probably faint clean away.)

Most Nubians and Nation-of-Islamites agree that "the white man is the devil", and some ascribe mystic powers to the dark skin pigment, Melanin. Such beliefs carry Hitler-like overtones, but are not always taken very seriously. Nubians enjoy the society of white people above all others, and hector them roguishly for hours, in a winsome way, expecting and usually receiving praise for doing so. Some Nation-of-Islamites, in England, have convinced themselves that the white man really *is* the devil. Instead of making them ferocious, this belief very naturally causes them to feel timid and nervous when in the presence of white people.

Shame over a past of slavery is the great stumbling block of Black History. Non-political West Indians and Black British share this unease. Church-goers of an older generation usually admire white people, and can scarcely credit the way that English slave-owners and traders evidently behaved.

Snubbed by a haughty West African, one Jamaican in London turned to another and said, "Why should he think he's better than me, just 'cos his ancestors could run faster than mine?" Such a remark is unusual, yet over and over again I have heard Jamaicans tell their children, as school holidays draw to an end, "Free paper burn now!" This saying refers to the freedom-certificate once granted to a freed slave, a piece of paper that could be destroyed at any moment and its holder returned to servitude.

A primary school in Harlesden, with a boisterous Irish headmistress, once held a Caribbean Carnival. Afterwards the Head switched off the Harry Belafonte records and addressed the assembled West Indian parents and children with these words.

"Why do Caribbean people have Carnival? (No answer.) All the grown ups will know the answer. What great event happened in 1833?"

Total silence. No grown-ups knew the answer.

"Why, the Abolition of Slavery!" the headmistress burst out triumphantly.

"Oh, right!" cried one young mother defiantly, a Nation of Islam sympathiser and neighbour of mine. All the other parents looked shocked. Almost in unison they picked up their bags and left, still in silence. Open-mouthed, the headmistress watched them go. Slavery, abolished or otherwise, is not a popular subject in Black Britain. (Incidentally, the Trinidad carnival began as a slave owner's festival, a last fling before Lent. Slaves and their descendants later took it over and added an African flavour.)

Life among the Nubians: On a visit to my childhood haunts in Islington, I called on a Jamaican friend, Mrs. Farmer. She and her grown-up son, Christopher, were both criticising Nigerians. When they had finished, tired but happy, Nigerians had not got a leg to stand on. Chris then offered to introduce me to a friend of his, who lived just down the road.

This friend proved to be Alan Mitchell, a "graphic novelist" who writes speech-balloon dialogue for a cartoon strip in *The Alarm*, the premier Nubian magazine. A kindly man, Mitchell welcomed us to his luxurious flat, and within seconds he and Christopher were deeply immersed in the Land of Punt. I had not realised until then that Chris had entered the Punt phase, and it was certainly odd to hear the same man who had condemned all Nigerians as rascals half an hour earlier now talking as if all Africans were demi-gods. Both Chris and Mitchell had recently discovered Fraser's *Golden Bough* and discussed it with wild enthusiasm. They also quoted the Bible a great deal, and had searched it for Nubian prophecies.

"My parents came from the island of St. Lucia", Mitchell told me. "But I was born over here."

"Do you consider yourself English?" I asked.

He jumped up as if shot, and roundly declared himself to be an African.

"I see no difference between West Indians, Black British and Africans!" he declared. "We are all Africans, no matter where we happen to be."

Part Seven. Black History, Black Crime and Black Triumphalism

There is a tenuous link between falsified Black History and crime — tenuous, because so many young men of every hue and background today jump at any excuse to justify wrongdoing.

I have heard, on a television documentary, predatory black youth in Watts, L.A., declare in ominous tones: "We used to be *kings* in Africa."

Exactly the same words are often used by those Black English youth who look to Watts for inspiration in clothes, music, drugs and crime. The inference is, that as white people have robbed black people of a priceless birthright, individual black people who rob white people are not really robbing them at all, but recovering their own property. Black History that condemns all white people as slave raiders easily becomes a licence to rob. Masai tribesmen on the East African plains used to believe that the Supreme Being poured all the cows of the world into Masai country as a gift for His Chosen People (the Masai). Therefore when Masai warriors go cattle raiding, they are not stealing but recovering their own property. All non-Masai cattle *must* have been stolen, as in ancient times all the world's wealth belonged to the Masai.

Too much emphasis on the glories of ancient Africa has resulted in a vague "muggers' philosophy" of "getting back our own." Black Power writers sometimes glamorise youthful robbers as "street warriors."

Most "street crime" in British cities is carried out by gleeful bands of children, of all colours. Not until the age of eighteen do young criminal boys grow philosophical. Some find a worthwhile philosophy and give up crime, others may seize on an ideology that "explains" and excuses the robbers' way of life.

While the link between Black History and Black Crime cannot be proved, the myth of the African Lost Paradise undeniably has helped in the creation of a brash new-rich Black British type of Black Triumphalism. Scorning their humble, hard-working West Indian immigrant parents, some rich "black conscious" Black Britons have "invented themselves" as a super-fashionable Master Race. Such young people take their styles from Black America and their history straight from Africa, as served up by fashionable historians and pre-historians.

"Prehistory", being unknown, or "pre-history", is a field that offers enormous scope to the imaginative. White English and American scientists have not only invented evolving birds, animals and reptiles, with the odd toe-bone as "evidence", but are now adept at discovering Cradles of Mankind. The latest Cradle, in fashion for the past thirty years, is Africa. Popular science blandly declares that the world began with a Big Bang and that human beings first appeared in Africa. Apparently the Supreme Being tipped His cradle over into the Olduvai Gorge in East Africa, where its fossilised occupants have been discovered by the white Leakey tribe of Kenya.

Nubian-minded black people in England and America swelled with pride on learning that the first humans were Africans. "*You* came from *us*", some declared to bewildered white people, who weren't sure whether a compliment or an insult was intended.

As always, there is another side to the Black Pride coin, and that is White Pride. To the Black-Proud Nubian, the first men in Africa were godlike beings in a Garden of Eden, while to the archaeologist Leakey they were ape-men. Leakey's First Man and First Woman of Africa were not, in their discoverer's

estimation, Adam and Eve, but a pair of small hairy apes —
"Zinjanthropi". Glancing at so-called "reconstructions" of those
apes, a man of White Pride would fall into the sub-Darwinian
notion of apes evolving into Negroes, or halfmen, and Negroes
evolving into White Men, or Proper People.

(Modern Africans in Mozambique have legends of "pygmy
ape men" known as "agogwe" who allegedly still live among
colonies of baboons. Since Leakey's fossils have been found in
baboon colonies, and date, some now believe, from historic times,
it could be that those Africans in Mozambique know what they're
talking about.)

Wherever Nubian book and craft shops flourish, Nation of
Islam-ites recruit and Black Theatres put on Black Plays, there
the brash super-fashionable image of Black Triumphalism can
be found. Where Pentecostal corner-churches and shop-front
churches flourish, something humble can be found, perhaps with
a flavour of Real Africa. As I write, the centres of Black
Triumphalism in London are Hackney and Brixton, with an
offshoot in the library at Willesden Green.

Black Triumphalists wear expensive clothes, with lots of gold,
and if female, lots of gaps between the clothing. They are not
low-life, but high-life, for their loud-voiced super-confidence wins
them both grants and bank loans (depending on whether they
have Blackademe-type jobs or are company directors). Nevertheless, there is a merging point between low life and high, as
drug peddlers and call-girls can also be wealthy and aggressive.
Triumphalists march confidently around, from Nubian Craft
Fairs to Black Theatre Workshops, elbowing others off the pavement.

What do Black Triumphalists *want*? Most of all to get rich.
They have two literary mouthpieces — *The Voice* newspaper,
and *The Alarm* magazine. Both are concerned in the creation of
a new Black British people, arisen as a fierce phoenix from the
ashes of a dove.

The Voice, under the tutelage of star-columnist Tony Sewell, urges the Black British to emulate the most crassly new-rich Black Americans. Most young people need little urging, as their baseball caps and T-shirts are covered in names of American baseball and football teams, "black" universities and cities where Black Americans are supposed to thrive. Martin Luther King's declamation "Free at Last!" is no longer seen, in England and America, as part of the great Christian's *dream*, but as solid reality. Black Americans are millionaires, just as Africans are Egyptian gods.

The Alarm, however, is alarmed at the "Americanising" trend, and believes strongly that the Black British should regard themselves as godlike Africans. One of the most readable parts of the magazine is the dialogue between two fictional Black Britons, Danny Dollar and Asher Africa. D. Dollar aspires to be a Black American, Asher Africa to be a Nubian African. Both are not so far apart in their views as might be supposed, as Danny Dollar's Black America omits the Deep South from its history and also plumes itself as godlike and African. At any rate, the writer clearly assumes that English black people have to be American or African. No one seems to think that most Black Britons are English people with a Caribbean past. The West Indies and its hard-working immigrant peoples have been thrown into the dustbin of True History, the kind of history that nobody wants.

Black Triumphalists have made an East End music hall, the Hackney Empire, a place of their own. Here Black Plays are performed weekly, all guaranteed to fill black people with the well-known "self-esteem." Why anyone needs to have "self-esteem" poured into him in the huge quantities prescribed by Black Triumphalists and their allies, I cannot think. Such esteem comes from a Pandora's box, for it is easier to give people self-esteem than it is to take it back again. If I could think of a way of ridding the world of self-esteem based on skin colour, I would do it.

At the Hackney Empire (all seats booked by credit card number, please) horrendously brash talent shows are put on, where every singer, musician or comedian who harks back to the days of decent cosiness in England or the West Indies, is roared mercilessly from the stage.

When I last passed by the Hackney Empire, edging nervously around aggressive young women dressed in strips of black leather and silver glitter, I gave a child in a pushchair a friendly nod. To my surprise, the three year old infant said, in clear bell-like tones, "I don't like you. I don't like people like you. You're horrible."

Such remarks are so unusual among children that I realised the little mite had learned colour-consciousness from its Triumphalist parents. Hackney leads London in Black Triumphalism, but may soon be overtaken by Willesden Green with its Black Conscious Self-Esteem-Filled library and arts complex. In the past, picturesque Mock Tudor Willesden Green library was staffed by querulous librarians who seemed alarmed by hefty, lounging-but-harmless black teenagers. Perhaps as a reaction against this, the council had the whole place pulled down and rebuilt, at enormous cost, as a shrine to Nubianism.

A disagreeable atmosphere of Black Triumphalism hangs over the library, with its Nubian Talent Night, Nubian Craft Fair and other delights. Black History has all but ousted the non-Black History books in the reference library. I once eavesdropped as a big young man with glasses held his noisy friends enthralled with jeers at white people. When the hoots of laughter had died down, the young people settled down to discuss the future *Alarm* mag, which had its birth in the library. It would be interesting to find out whether or not library funds have been spent on the magazine.

Near Harlesden, last week, I saw two Triumphalist girls, with a tiny boy in the usual push chair, stamping along the middle of the pavement ahead of me, talking at the tops of their voices. A slender white girl tried to pass them, and to my surprise and hers, one of the pushchair girls gave her a great purposeful bump from the hip, which left her staggering. Such behaviour is so unusual in a neighbourhood where West Indians and English people seem particularly friendly, that the bumped girl looked stunned. Pulled along by my dog, I tried to give the Triumphalists a wide berth.

"That dog looks just like Charlie", the little boy in the push-chair piped up, in a sweet, innocent voice.

"Yes! Except Charlie doesn't have *sex* with his *owner!*" the mother shouted fiercely.

This was a classic case of Black Triumphalism, I mused. "Bump Days" began in Atlanta, Georgia, in the late 'sixties, as an offshoot of the Black Power movement. Young black people would walk along in a group, and bump every white person they saw out of the way. At least the Harlesden girls' Bump Day seemed to be a private occasion between the two of them. It would be a bit thick if *all* the young people around went a-bump-ing, the air thick with cries of "Happy Bump Day to You!"

As for the slur against the moral character of my dog, it echoes an accusation more commonly made by Africans against ex-pat dog owners. Dogs are looked on with fear and scorn by most Africans and many West Indians, and for those who jeer at white people, the white man's liking for his dog is the most obvi-ous target for dislike. The only explanation for the affection be-tween Man and Dog to some Africans is the one given by the two Triumphalist girls.

(Incidentally, many village African dog owners name their pets after personal enemies, so that they can abuse the dog and the enemy at the same time, like this:- "Curse you, Asare, you flea-bitten filth-eating stinking son of a cur! Oh, not *you*, Asare, dear neighbour — I was talking to my dog! My greetings to all in your compound....." Slaves and sharecroppers in the Deep South sometimes named their mules after a "bossman", for the same reason.

Englishmen in Africa ought to think carefully before naming their dogs — one colonial type in Jomo Kenyatta's Kenya was put on trial in High Court for calling his dog "Jomo." He was acquitted when the dog answered to "Joe".)

Harking back to the girls in Harlesden, I saw the same two, later that day, in the High Street. A diffident semi-brainwashed man emerged from the Nation of Islam shop and sold them a newspaper. They greeted the flattered man with noisy rapture, delighted at having the Nation of Islam in their midst. Not far away, stuck to a lamp post, was a tattered advertisement for a Nubian lecture on Black History, which ended in these words: "Do not be fooled by the European concept of 'God.' 'God' is only an anagram of 'Dog', and a Dog is Man's Best Friend. That is, some kinds of men, the pale kind."

Part Eight. What is History?

The word "history" just means "a story", but in the modern usage, it is assumed to mean "a true story" or "a true account from the earliest known times to the present day." An account of what? There are histories of objects, inventions and everything under the sun, but to the old-fashioned schoolboy, "history" means the history of nations and of his own nation in particular.

With the emergence of Black History, the question I posed in Part One is raised: Does history have to be true, or is its purpose to make a people feel proud of themselves and of all their past achievements? I am fairly proud to be English, when considering some of the things olden-day English people have done. If, however, I were to feel proud, or full of self-esteem, over *everything* English people have done, I would have had to have learned a fictitious or at best heavily-edited history. Such a history is being foisted on the children and grandchildren of West Indian immigrants. At the very same time, English history for white children is being phased out, treated as an unimportant and inconsequential part of "Humanities.'"

"Black History" is as yet *encouraged* but not exclusively taught in English schools. "Black Heroes" have their pictures all over school walls, and children are expected to pick an appropriately-coloured "hero" and write essays on him or her, usually from material gathered at the local public library. The more fantastic or "Nubian" side of Black History is taught at Centres, evening classes, colleges and Saturday schools for children. Official or municipal England is greatly in favour of Black History, role models, self-esteem and so on, and encourages it by grants and other favours. "Higher-up" or governmental England approves of such history and esteem because it is vaguely felt that black people must be occupied with something or they might riot. But my opinion is that history ought to be truthful, and a made-up history that blames all ills on the white race produces selfish people and criminals. The fact that some of the criminals may enjoy considerable self-esteem fails to cheer me.

True history, however distressing it may be to read of the centuries of slave-trading, makes an exciting story. Human nature seems to require a story to have a happy ending, which can be done by closing a written account at a given time. However, as history is self-written, since things go on happening, this presents difficulties. English history made a very satisfying story when the books ended just before the outbreak of the Great War. If the book ended in 1918 or 1945, the story remained a great one. But if the book has to end in 1996, a bad time for England, the story seems to have no proper ending at all. My schoolboy history books had the Rise of the Empire as the happy ending.

Intellectuals of my own generation, born in the nineteen forties, looked forward to the Ending of the Empire as a Happy Ending indeed. When wars, famines and dictatorships resulted, our sense of England's Mission to End Empire was destroyed. Many of the former colonies have now settled down as ordinary countries, but they are not earthly paradises, as was once expected. Both the pro and the anti-Empire factions in Britain have received an *unhappy* ending, and so in pique seem to have abolished English History.

The adventure story that is History has to have characters, and in English History the characters are the nations. Our hero, or central figure, is England, and her circle of neighbours and acquaintances are Germany, Russia, France, Spain, America and so on. Sometimes all are friends, but sometimes they tend to quarrel. Often they are good, but more often they are *very naughty*. England, the hero of English History, changes character over the years. In one century, she does a good thing, in the next a bad thing. She can be generous, she can be mean or wasteful. Here she is kind, there she is proud and selfish. It would be nice to suppose that she is a Christian. Just as England changes character, in this Little Arthur's Child View of History, so she can (if she wishes) change colour.

Since the above view of History, the child's view and the adult's view in certain moods, is the one that decides the reader's place in the world and decides who he is, the time has come for a decision. Is the hero to be the International Black Man or the Englishman? "Black Britain", as a separate entity, could be defined as "People who want to be Black Americans." "Black Britain" demands a glorious Straight-from-Africa History, as peddled to Black Americans. An Englishman calls for English History, which now must *include* people of various colours. If some of these people have a non-English background, then so have the English aristocracy (French), the British Royal Family (German) and the English white working class (also German, hence their love for Royalty). Even the Celts can be traced to India, and their dark-haired sub-section to North Africa. English History needs a Happy Ending, and I would suggest not the Rise of Empire, nor the Loss of Empire, but the Coming Home of Empire.

My belief that History ought to be true is mitigated, to some extent, by my belief in the importance to children of mythological episodes. Canute and the waves, Alfred and the cakes, Bruce and the spider — these *may* be true stories and ought to be given the benefit of the doubt. They give history the flavour of folklore, and prevent it from becoming dull. After all, history *is* a folk's lore, being nothing if not traditional. Historians should strive for the truth, but the truth is an elusive grail. If you worry *too* much over what is true, you won't be able to tell a story at all.

To my mind, the story of a person, or a tribe or a nation is worth telling, but the story of a *race* is not. How could Kenyatta have written about the Kikuyu, Kulet about the Masai and

Achebe about the Ibo if they had only been allowed to refer to "black people"? Black History, seen from Blackademe's American perspective, cannot break up into myriad histories of tribes, but has to refer only to "black people", "Africans" or (by way of variety) "Afrikans."

In the Deep South in slavery times, and to some extent today, the Negroes saw themselves as Israelites in bondage to Pharaoh. "Go Down Moses", a classic spiritual, expressed this feeling very well. Modern Blackademe, with its anti-Southern bias, has stood the spiritual on its head by calling on black people to identify with the oppressor Pharaoh ("We were *kings* in Egypt....."). Not surprisingly, given the thorough grounding in the Bible enjoyed by most American Negroes, this switch-over to Old King Pharaoh's side is usually accompanied by anti-Semitism.

There was a time, not very long ago, in the Middle Ages, when English history, as taught, resembled the Nubian excesses of Black History. Geoffrey de Monmouth (1100-1154), the archdeacon of Llandaff, near Cardiff, wrote a very influential book, "Historia Britonum." In its modern English translation, the book is lively and readable, and presents history as a series of myths, folktales and invention. Welsh, English and Normans alike felt flattered to learn that the British were the descendants of Trojans. According to Geoffrey de Monmouth, the Fall of Troy to the wily gift-bearing Greeks led some Trojans to flee to England on the advice of their gods. Led by Brute, who gave his name to Britain, these fugitives colonised our island and gave it a prestigeworthy link to classical antiquity.

Lacking a very glorious history, twelfth century Britons seized on Geoffrey's writings with glee. Now they could hold their heads up, and even acquire self-esteem, when others spoke of Rome, Athens and Troy. Did not Brute found London and call the city New Troy? Well, no, he did not, but few could swallow such a bitter pill until the Renaissance. By then the *true* story of England had gathered some credit to its name, and Geoffrey's yarn gradually faded in importance. Today, Geoffrey de Monmouth is known as a proto-folklorist who unearthed some interesting King Arthur legends. As Black Britons start to distinguish themselves, the fictitious side to English Black History will surely fade away.

Most state-educated white English people under forty years of age know nothing of their history, discarded with shame as "all bad", riddled with militarism, slavery and imperialism. As a result, people don't feel English and seize eagerly at any other name, be it "Brit", "white man" or "Arsenal supporter." Possibly the low British sperm count can be linked to the decline of English History. A discredited people with no history, the white English may simply have given up the will to live. A glance in any pushchair will show that the non-white sperm count is as high as ever.

Knowing no history, the white English cannot counter-attack the diatribes of Nubian historians, since for all they know the Nubians are telling the truth.

Lack of a sense of Englishness has had a curious side effect — many children in London schools may know that they are black, but *they do not know what country they live in.* I discovered this curious fact when teaching English to the children of immigrants in "multi-racial Brent." Some young people as old as twelve knew only that they lived in London. When asked what country London was in, they guessed wildly — "America!" — "No, Russia!"

In a Sunday School class, I overheard an elderly Jamaican lady tell two bright little boys of six and seven: "You are not Jamaicans, because you were born in England. You were born in England, so what does that make you?"

After a moment of puzzled thought, both boys burst out, "I know! We're Irish! We were born in England, so we're Irish!"

Probably the only white boys in the local primary school were of Irish stock, hence the misunderstanding. Children of Indian ancestry seemed particularly confused as to what country they lived in. Many had been taught smatterings of Black History by white teachers — the Lives of Bob Marley, Malcolm X and Mary Seacole. If the white English would only assert, with all due modesty, that they are English and live in England, then the brown and black English would get the idea. Possibly, some of the white working class are *pleased* at being English, but keep quiet about it, in case black people should want to be English too. This brings me to:

Part Nine. The Truth Shall Set You Free

To the English-born Black Triumphalist, on his or her way to a brassy night-club in Hackney, West Indians of the nineteen fifties immigrant generation are an embarrassment. Supposedly duped into coming to England, their only purpose was to beget rich confident Black Britons. "Windrush-minded" Black Historians are less harsh in their attitudes, and smile with affectionate pity for their parents or grandparents who "came over in the 'fifties".

"The 'Windrush generation' were duped by a British recruitment campaign", is an opinion often heard. This is an attempt at explaining the inexplicable, since Black Triumphalists cannot understand why black people should want to go to a white people's country.

What "recruitment campaign"? Some invitations to work in Britain seem to have been circulated in Barbados, but few if any such leaflets appeared in Jamaica or Trinidad, let alone West Africa. While "first generation immigrants" are still alive, the truth may not be hard to find. Why search the rifled tombs of Egyptian kings for your history when the truth may be on the lips of your own grandmother?

Mind you, people who live through momentous times are not always the best judge of what has happened to themselves. Often confused, they later seize on a popular interpretation of the events concerned. Some West Indian parents felt so shocked by their introduction to England that they kept silent about the past, telling nothing to their British-born children. Later arrivals, who came in the early 'sixties, are far more open about their experiences. This may be because news of what England was like had by then filtered back to the Caribbean, so that the reality came as less of a surprise. Those who came in the early 'sixties found Africans and West Indians already well-established here. Dancehalls and churches rang with "back home" accents. 'Sixties people found it comparatively easy to settle in Britain, yet far from answering a recruitment campaign, they came in the teeth of "Send them back" propaganda and looming anti-immigration laws.

As I remember it, from my schoolboy days in the "African League", every boat-load of West Indians that arrived in Britain was met by eager con-men from West Africa or Trinidad, out to fleece and bamboozle the newcomers. Almost certainly, similar con-men thrived in the Caribbean, touting hire-purchase boat tickets with assurances that "Everyone in England is going mad trying to recruit West Indians to work in high-paid jobs!"

This might explain the plight of my friend Virginia Farmer, who spent her first night in London shivering on a station bench as she "waited for the man to come and tell me where to live and give me a job".

Like a Gold Rush, the fever to go to England to get rich and see the Queen, the immigration urge may simply have "come over" people.

"In nineteen fifty three, just after the Coronation, the Queen came to Jamaica", a friend of mine from that island told me admiringly. "She liked it there! We saw her walking about, a beautiful tall young lady. Soon after that, we were allowed to go to England."

This belief in a Royal invitation forms a parallel with the slavery-time notion that Queen Victoria had personally set the slaves free immediately upon her accession to the throne. In reality, a long-drawn out struggle against slavery had at last reached fruition in the British Empire just as Victoria's reign began. As ever, folklore merges into history.

"Windrushian-historians" tend to forget that Jamaicans and other West Indians had long felt the call to travel and see the world as sailors, fishermen and migrant workers. Plenty of middle-aged West Indians now living in English cities had their first taste of Abroad in the plantations of the southern states of America.

"I remember working in Florida in the nineteen sixties", a middle-aged Jamaican, Mr. Barnet, told me. "We were picking oranges and cutting sugar cane with machetes. You know, we had to watch out for the rattlesnakes! Some o' them were five feet long, with a tail that goes 'brrr'! to warn you. They would be there in that cane, curled up, tail going 'brrr'! Dangerous, man, I tell you!"

At a bus stop, I recently fell into conversation with a tall, strong-looking elderly West Indian. He wore a peaked cap adorned with the Confederate flag, emblem of the white Southern rebels who fought so bravely for slavery.

"Yes, I've been to the American South", the old man told me proudly. "Back in the 'fifties, I worked on contract in Florida, cutting sugar cane. It was not like you and me might cut it, but very rough!" (He mimed seizing a large bunch of cane in one hand.) "You has to cut a whole bunch, and them does leave the cane for two or three years to grow real, real high. Then I got sent to Wisconsin to pick apple, an' after that to Curacao, an island near Venezuela, to work blasting in the quarries. I came here to England in nineteen sixty two."

"That was quite a good year", I mentioned, meaning that the tribulations of the 'fifties were then beginning to fade.

"Yes, it was warm that year", he replied easily, and stepped onto a bus.

Reminiscences of the 'fifties from West Africans in England are surprisingly hard to find in print. "Oral historians" tend to seek out West Indians who fit into the "everyman" pattern beloved by tape-recordists. Like some West Indians, West Africans often find it hard to explain their own bizarre experiences.

My stepfather, for example, was secretary of the "African League" throughout the nineteen fifties. He believed that his campaign to end the British Empire was violently opposed by the British government. When the so-called "imperialist government" abolished the Empire of its own accord, the perplexed "African League" also disbanded.

Believing, in spite of all evidence to the contrary, that he and his "League" were involved in a Struggle, my stepfather was dumbfounded when an upper class civil servant, Henry Hopkinson, called at our humble home to discuss the forthcoming End of Empire on an official level. Hopkinson (later Lord Colyton) held the view that, with no Empire, it would be easy to ban coloured immigrants from coming to Britain. From being British citizens, black people would become Foreigners. Baffled at finding himself on the same side as "the enemy", my stepfather had recourse to a day of illness.

I have read a published account of West African life in 'fifties London, a Nigerian paperback called *Victims of Imperialism*. It bears no relation at all to the truth, through no fault save that of the understandable confusion of the author. According to the book, the author and several other young men had been sent to England from Nigeria under the auspices of the British Communist Party. The Party was supposed to send them on to East Germany, there to study at a Soviet-style university. Somehow or other, the young people found themselves holed up in the room of a Nigerian Communist called Edward. Nobly, Edward protected them from Colonial Office spies and other imperialists who wished to capture them, lock them up forever and then torture them. Whenever the author went out, sinister imperialists spied on him or gave chase. Shaking with terror, he eventually reached East Germany, completed his studies and returned to Nigeria. His East German experiences, part of the Happy Ending, were dismissed in two or three lines.

My mother knew Edward and had met some of the young people crammed into his room and fed on a diet of rancid rice.

Edward was no cook, but topped up the rice saucepan at intervals. The young people were supposed to be the children of miners killed during a strike at Enugi in Nigeria. *Daily Worker* readers responded well to a fund raised to send the orphans to East Germany. Edward had been entrusted with the task of receiving the orphans and sending them on to the Soviet paradise. To his dismay, the white Communist high-ups did not pay him for his trouble.

Never mind, the parents of the "orphans" had paid him to provide an education for their children, who were no relation to the miners at all. He kept them all in one room, on short rations, while he tried ineffectually to get tickets to the East German Republic. It was Edward's fear of arrest for fraud, ill-treatment of minors and other offences that led him to invent ghostly colonial officials bent on torture and murder. How else could he keep the boys indoors? As it was, he *did* get into some police trouble over the incident, concerning a girl of fourteen kept behind after the others had gone. This is *not* the sort of Black History that usually gets into books.

Robert Burns, the Scottish poet, once contemplated fleeing to Jamaica after he made a girl pregnant. Similarly, a Jamaican once recounted his reason for emigration as follows:

"I was doing well at school, but me and this girl were having a love affair. The girl was a good scholar, and her family were very proud of her. One day I heard a fearful yelling and shouting at my girlfriend's yard, and she crying. Then I saw *all* her relations go marching toward my own house! I know what happen, a baby come, so I *jumped* over the wall and *run* to Kingston where a friend find me a boat to England. I can never go back!"

However, most tales of immigration have a nobility and a pathos to them, that belie the Black Triumphalist sneers of "dupes" and the Nubians' claim of African Royal blood in all its arrogancy. Why should we be better than our fathers? It is more likely that our fathers are better than us. If your grandfather tells you that he came here as a British West Indian, why not believe him instead of dreaming of an African neverland? From British Empire to Hackney Empire is a downward step, in my opinion. If you *really* want to be African, why not listen to the elders? Many a grandfather has an interesting tale to tell.

"… I arrive at Southampton off the boat in nineteen fifty seven, and set out to find my friend's address in Kilburn. It was winter-time, you know. There I was, in the freezing cold, wearing my tropical shirt. It was so cold, I wondered how people could live in England, as it seemed impossible to endure such cold. How could they live?

"Finally I reach Kilburn, but my friend was not in! He was out at work all day. So I had nowhere to go, I just stood shivering in the doorway. I couldn't see no coloured people at all. At long last, a friendly white lady lets me into the house and into me friend room. I doesn't know how to light the fire or light the stove, so I still cold, and can't cook or eat. The white lady show me a shop, and I try to buy milk, but I got confused and went away. You see, I thought you could eat and drink in the shop, like I was used to in Jamaica, not have to take the carton of milk away.

"When my friend came back at night, was I pleased! Day by day, I learn how to buy coal and light the fire. I got a job in one o' the aluminium foundries they have at Park Royal in them days, and I work in the foundries till they all close. Never went back home at all."

English cold, in those pre-central heating days, was a force to be reckoned with. Shivering newcomers were surprised to see their own breath condensing in the air "like dragon smoke from my mouth!" Many rejoiced at first that England had so many factories and such a need for work! The only smoking chimneys they had ever seen before were those of factories and rum distilleries, so they mistook the rows of houses for factories. Soon they would be living in rooms in those terraced houses, saving money and sending it "back home."

My tall young friend Sister Dorothy told me how she felt

when her mother in England unexpectedly sent for her. Many a child, cared for by a grandmother in the West Indies, suddenly received a ticket through the post and was summarily despatched to parents in England. Such involuntary immigrants now form a middle-aged generation, not quite Black British, not quite West Indian.

Like many Caribbean people, Sister Dorothy is a born-again Christian and member of a Pentecostal church. Members of such churches are usually untroubled by yearnings for an earthly place to belong, whether it be a Black Nation, Black Britain, sitcom America or a mythical Africa. They will tell you that they belong to Jesus, and at the drop of a tambourine will sing country and western hymns such as "This World is Not My Home, I'm Just Passing Through."

Totally uninterested in "Black History", such church members are often knowledgeable in *real* history along with folklore, as affection and respect for old people is very much a part of church life. Knowing little about Africa, and oblivious of "Black Movements" other than Holy Ghost dancing, the church people *unconsciously* carry a little Africa everywhere they go. Strong links of custom hold them to churches and families in the West Indies.

When I first met Sister Dorothy she was a secretary in a Barclays Bank. Apolitical to a fault, she felt very nervous about anti-apartheid protesters, who at that time occasionally stormed into Barclays for impromptu protests. As an English bank with branches in South Africa, Barclays helped black people everywhere by employing them. This cut no ice with the protesters, one of whom had once threatened Sister Dorothy.

"I do not see myself as a secretary, or as black, but as a child of God", she told me seriously. "Me and Yvonne, my sister, were brought up in Barbados by our grandmother. Everyone always told us 'One day you will go in an aeroplane to England and live with your mother.'

"From the earliest I remember, I was always thinking about

my mother. 'Will I know her?' I thought. I would pray to God that I would know my mother when I saw her, and that she'd know me. That day dawned, and we were put on the 'plane to be met at the other end by our mother! I was five years old.

"No sooner did I see my mother than I knew her at once, as if we had never been parted! Yet we had parted when I was a baby and couldn't even talk! When we got to our house, a man was there in a London Transport guard's uniform. I didn't know anything about the Underground, so I thought he was a policeman!

"I'm your new daddy', he said,

"I thought '*Uh*?' I didn't even know I had an *old* daddy. We had never thought about fathers back at my grandmother's house in Barbados. But our daddy was really nice to us from the first, so friendly and jolly. He took us straight away to Trafalgar Square and let us climb on the lions. But to our surprise, we had two new sisters in London, Shirley and Anna.

"Anna was upset at first, when me and Yvonne came along. 'She's not your mummy!' she told us, but we soon put *her* right! Now we all get along fine."

A baby brother soon followed. All the family lived in the same minute terraced house until a couple of years ago, when Dorothy, Yvonne and Anna moved into separate flats nearby. The Barbadian-born girls and the English-born still seem like two sets of two sisters in one family.

Sister Dorothy's story, seemingly commonplace now, is a piece of real history. In her church, the congregation invoke "The Holy Spirit of Truth, the Comforter." Somewhere along the line, perhaps because American Blackademe cannot accept accurate descriptions of slavery days, the spirit of Truth has fled from Black History. Most seekers after Black History reject Truth and seek comfort through fantasy. Individual reminiscences, in all their homely lack of pomp, are not History as the Black Historian understands the term. The creation and glorification of Black Britain apparently calls for a *false* history, and no other kind will do.

Despite the fact that the false history links Black Britons to Black Americans in Los Angeles, then harks straight back to the days of the Pharoahs in Ancient Egypt, it is distinctly Jamaican in tone. Black Britons who do not feel at least *sub*-Jamaican, and have no tie with any country save Britain, sometimes tread a lonely path. They may be told "You're not a *true* black" by black people, and "You're not English" by white people. Some leave England and find solace in the backpacking world of international bohemia. Others become vehemently "black", and peddle Black History and general "blackness" to fascinated white people. White people often expect something wild and exotic from black people, and "Englishness" is not exotic enough for England.

If there is a romance about England, it is an historical romance, and black people have now become a part of the True History of England. Truth is fascinating for its own sake, not for the sake of personal, national or racial vanity.

Romance from Africa will never be lacking. The immigrants of the nineteen fifties and 'sixties have brought a sense of African-ness that has spread out beyond the realms of Black Britain, in many homely, delightful and amusing ways.

When a West African villager or market woman is mildly surprised or amused at some piece of gossip or information, she or he exclaims "Eh eh!", with a slightly throaty intonation. This "eh eh!" has been carried over to the West Indies without any change whatsoever, a universal Africanism. In America, it may have evolved into the well-known "Uh-oh!", uttered by all races. In English cities, young white people now unselfconsciously cry "Eh eh!" with the best of them.

Not long ago, I visited the Bashir family in Handsworth, Birmingham. Mr. and Mrs. Bashir were born in Pakistan, but their English-born daughters Tasveer and Tasleem seem Jamaico-Brummie through and through. Both girls were surprised to see me.

"Eh eh!" they exclaimed in unison.

Now married, Tasveer and Tasleem may go to Pakistan and take their "Eh ehs" with them. To me, the Long March of the "Eh Eh" is a fascinating piece of linguistic history. Not Black History, White History or Brown History, but simply History as such.

Eh eh! You know it's the truth!

Afterword

Since this book was completed, Willesden Library has grown less aggressively "black" and now has a large selection of English History books on its shelves.

Thanks to the efforts of dedicated educationalists, state secondary schools now teach History as a subject of its own — another recent change. For over ten years, at secondary school level, History and Geography had been submerged in the pseudo-subject of Humanities. As matters stand, most pupils can now take History or Geography for GCSE, but not both. A mass of history books are now pouring into children's libraries and trickling into schools. So far, few if any of these books are hardbacks — most are flexible brightly-coloured bound pamphlets. Even so, they are an improvement on the photo-copied and loosely stapled Information Packs of two years ago. The format of the books resembles that of popular women's magazines — no lengthy chapters, but titbits of information scattered about a page, enclosed in boxes, each with a *Daily Mirror*-like headline. Loud colours, with lots of red, distract the eye from taking in details of prints and photographs.

Most strange of all are the 'Sources', small boxed-off extracts of historical writings by various hands, some items dating from the period under scrutiny. The school child is supposed not be learning history, but to be an historian, quoting from 'sources'. Of course 'sources' not specially provided by the book's author and left handily around would not count for good marks. "Working from sources" has become a quiz game. Which source is correct and which is biased? In modern History, the scholar quickly realises that biased sources are labelled *Daily Mail*. Sources from pre-*Mail* days are obviously meant to be suspect if derived from the writings of wealthy or powerful men. On one occasion, I have seen a chunk of *Little Arthur's English History*, the archetypal Victorian history book, quoted as a 'source' on the Tudor period.

'History videos', not books, are often shown to comprehensive pupils without comment from the teacher . Homework essays based on these films are often weird and wonderful to behold.

Even now, flashbacks from the days of 'Humanities' bedevil English History as taught in Comprehensive schools. Homework on 'the ozone layer' and 'global warming' suddenly intrudes on the Tudors, as do endless requests for home-researched essays on Martin Luther King, Gandhi and Malcolm X. Gandhi's criticisms of Hindu belief in Untouchables, child-marriage and the subjection of women have been swept aside, and he is presented as the champion of everything Indian. Similarly Martin Luther King is supposed by many teachers and writers of pop history for schoolboys to be a "black separatist" and opponent of white people, almost indistinguishable from Malcolm 'X'. Malcolm's conversion to historic non-racial Islam has also been written out of school history

I have dwelled at length on English History as taught in schools, partly because of changes made since the completion of my book, and partly because spurious Black History takes over when English History is not known. For the most part, Black History of the kind described in my book as a series of myths, is not taught in schools but hinted at in schools with coloured pupils, by wall posters and books left scattered around, not set.

Among adults, mythological Black History is spoken about more than it is read or written. Black American pundit, Leonard Jefferies, famous for his classification of humanity into Ice People and Sun People, appears never to have written a book, though he has contributed chapters to various collections of Black historical thoughts. His reputation rests on his lectures in American "black colleges". The typical believer in Black History in England is a devotee of 'phone in' radio rather than the printed page. He often believes, quite mistakenly, that his theories on "The Hidden Black Presence" appear with complete proof attached in the writings of historians Peter Fryer and Ziggi Alexander.

A word of explanation is due to British members of the Nation of Islam, the sect dominated in the USA by Louis Farrakhan. I call members of the Nation 'brainwashed' because after training at the Goldhawk Road headquarters they emerge wearing identical dress and speaking in identical acquired American accents. There is little if anything sinister in the Nation of Islam in Britain, and I have been treated very kindly by concerned staff in Nation bookshops. They are chiefly concerned for my feelings, in case these are hurt by my reading anti-white literature from America.

The Nation of Islam seems better versed in the Bible than in the Koran. They differ from avowedly Christian Africans, West Indians, and Black British in that they imagine that all the people mentioned in the Bible are black. Members of gospel-singing churches usually visualise Bible characters as white. (I imagine that most people in the Biblical Near East and North Africa are, and always have been, Brown.)

Now to the Hackney Empire, the music hall whose brash influence forms one of the themes of my book. So far I have been unable to speak to anyone at the Hackney Empire person to person — only person to answerphone. However the Cockney monologues on Empire answerphones make it clear that the Empire puts on as much "family entertainment" as it does "black entertainment". "Family" in East End context clearly means a traditional East End "Mum, Dad and the kids".

Black American ideas on family life do not apply to England, whether or not a belief in Black supremacy is involved.

From the early days of immigration, the nineteen forties, to to-day, a family of "Black British" children are likely to have a white mother and a black father. Sometimes the father lives else-where and seldom sees his children. All too often such children feel compelled by a white teacher's insistence on Black Pride, Self-Esteem and Never Forgetting your Roots into a Black Triumphalism in which their self-sacrificing mother can play no part save that of an embarrassment.

In a workmen's cafe in Kilburn, I sat at the same table as a harassed young mother and a lively brown toddler. A genial Irishman fell into conversation with the mother, and after a while enquired in a soft voice, "The dad is black?"

"Yes, heart and soul" the mother replied with great empha-sis, then sighed.

Can pride in being Black, like other forms of male pride, lead a man into ill-treating his wife? Can no virtues transcend the barrier of race? As I write, the "racial make up" of our cities is being changed by the arrival of hundreds of Somali families, most of them Moslems. These good-humoured intelli-gent people are Negroes yet untouched by fashionable black-ness. It will be interesting to see how ideas on race and religion are altered by their presence, once they are more established and can all speak English. They may, for all I know, form a bridge between West Indian and "Asian" Indian. Somaliland is close to the "Back to Africanists'" Ethiopia and Nubia. English Somalis are bound to make a change in Black Thought.

Bibliography

The Book of Glory of the Blacks Over the Whites, A V A I B A1 Johiy, 776-868 AD. Trans. Vincent Cornell. E.C.A. Associates, Chesapeake, New York, 1990.

This piece of Koranic apocrypha might be of historical interest but no serious commentary has been provided. It contains full page illustrations of Vincent Cornell, who resembles a dapper businessman, and seems a fair example of Land of Punt American Blackademe.

Little Arthur's History of England, Lady Callcott. Price 18d. John Murray, 1893.

The archtypal child's history book, never bettered. With a few small alterations it could be used in primary schools today. Chapter One begins "You know, my dear little Arthur, that the country you live in is called England" — information that would be of great value to many eleven year olds today.

In her introduction, "To Mothers"; Lady Callcott has this to say; "Let no one fear that to cultivate patriotism is to make men illiberal in feelings towards mankind in general. Is any man the worse citizen for being a good son, brother, or father, or husband? I am indeed persuaded that the well-grounded love of our own country is the best security for that enlightened philanthropy which is aimed at as the perfection of moral education."

Melanin 'n' Me, Beverly Crespo, A&B publishers, Brooklyn, 1996. A child's guide to the wonders of Mystic Melanin. Blackademe for infants.

Tropical Africa, Henry Drummond, Hodder and Stoughton, 1888.

Poetic descriptions of Southern Africa by a Scottish writer famed in his day for a style that combined mysticism with scientific fact. He describes Arab slave caravans from first hand observation, and calls on the West to stamp out this evil.

Staying Power, Peter Fryer, Pluto Press, 1984.

A best seller among the Black-conscious British, this book caused great excitement when it came out. It was seized on by the Hidden Black Presence school as proof of a continuous Black Community in England from the earliest times. This only goes to show that many of the Black-conscious British don't read books very thoroughly and tend to find in them what they want to find. Fryer lists every black person who has ever lived in Britain, as best as he is able, but is unable to prove the never failing growth of a Black community. Most of the black men whose existence he documents must have married English women. Few of these men were born in England. A similar book could have been written about Oriental visitors and servants in Britain, proving nothing at all except that Oriental visitors and servants have been here and left little trace.

An interesting book, *Staying Power* quotes eighteenth century posters advertising slaves for sale in England. These slaves had almost all been the property of returned planters from the Caribbean. Slavery in England in the eighteenth century forms a parallel, in my opinion, with polygamy in modern Britain. Polygamy is not an English custom and has no sanction of law, yet Eastern polygamists sometimes come to England with all their wives. This makes an ass of the law and no-one is quite sure what to do. However no new wives can be added, in this country, just as no free people in eighteenth century England could legally be enslaved.

Peter Fryer is a former Communist and *Daily Worker* reporter, still remembered in the party for his reports on the Hungarian uprising. *Staying Power* ends with a lyrical description of the

Brixton riots, presented as the apotheosis of Britain's Black community.

Pioneers in West Africa, Sir Harry Johnston. With eight coloured illustrations by the author. One of the Pioneers of Empire series, Blackie and Son, 1912.

Sir Harry Johnston is one of my heroes, and the eight coloured illustrations are a delight. How I wish this had been one of my history books at school! Sir Harry, an expert on African languages and wild life, describes Africans with affection but no sentimentality. Arab slave raids are described vividly and mention is made of a forest tribe who hated the English for ending the slave trade, their former livelihood. Johnston himself was an English imperial pioneer in Africa and did his bit to stamp out slavery. However, he is hated by many members of Nigeria's Ibo tribe for his treatment of King Jaja.

What they Never told you in History class, Indus Khamil Kush, D&J Book Distributors Inc, 21, Merrick Boulevarde, Lowelton, NY 11413, 1983.

Author of *The Missing Pages of His-Story*, Khamil Kush is yet another prosperous looking shiny-suited member of American Blackademe, to judge by his photograph. Possibly his baptismal name is not Khamil Kush. His re-interpretation of world and American history seems to show that white people are few on the ground.

Ancient and Modern Britons, David MacRitchie, Pine Hill Press, Inc, Freeman, South Dakota 57029. Two volumes. Copyright 1991 William Preston.

MacRitchie was an eminent Scottish historian, who wrote in the eighteen eighties. Long out of print, his books have, to our great good fortune, been reissued if not co-opted by American Blackademe. This is because of MacRitchie's belief, reprinted on the cover, that "make no mistake, the Picts were Blackamoors". The author makes a persuasive case that wild Scotland, in early times, was home to lawless tribes of indigenous coloured people. Resembling George Borrow in style and interests, MacRitchie writes about Picts, gypsies, broken clans and Hebridean islanders who lived in wigwams. These last are so well documented that I am now convinced that some ancient Scots were at least tawnimoors, or people who resembled Red Indians. I have long noted the affinity between Scotsmen, Gypsies and Redskins. I have met Cherokee Scotsmen in Tennessee, a newly created tribe proud of both strands of ancestry.

Scottish gypsies are fascinating people, highly intelligent and good humoured. Predatory tribes, like predatory animals, are often more intelligent than pastoral herbivores. When tamed they make excellent companions. MacRitchie has convinced me that "broken clans" of Scottish reivers led by haughty chiefs sometimes took to the road when their castles and peel towers were seized or destroyed. They joined or became gypsies. For decades, Romany gypsies scorn to marry outsiders — then they meet outsiders they like, and merge with a will. This happened with gypsies and East End Cockneys and in America with gypsies and American Indians. Perhaps the Scottish gypsies I met at Appleby Horse Fair were not only descendants of long ago Eastern Indians but also of Lowland Scottish Chiefs.

In a later book *Fairy Forts*, still out of print, MacRitchie recants his 'Picts were Black' theory and suggests instead that they were Lapps! It was the Black Pictish element in MacRitchie's books that has saved them for posterity. A modern member of American Blackademe, William Preston, has brought McRitchie to light and almost taken the credit for the Scotsman's discoveries. In his introduction, replete with absurdities, Preston seeks to prove that press-man Rupert Murdoch is black. Preston is proud of his own blackness, but seems to gleefully think Murdoch will be mortally offended by this charge. Should Murdoch take up Black Pride, Preston will be confounded.

The Lunatic Express — an Entertainment in Imperialism, Charles Miller, MacDonald & Co, 1971.

Obliged by the conventions of his time to portray the British

Empire with gentle amusement, the American author quickly drops this pose and writes with open admiration of British explorers and anti-slavery campaigners of late Victorian and Edwardian times. Only with the annexation of East Africa by European powers was the Arab slave trade destroyed. Like myself, Miller is somewhat pro-District Officer and anti-Settler. Much of this book is devoted to the construction of the Uganda railway, which opened East Africa, for better or worse, to the outside world. Thanks to Miller I now realise that many philanthropic Arabs in past centuries rescued slaves from captivity.

The Naming of an Afrikan Child, K Mokbabaka, Ankh Arts, P.O. Box 578243.(1991).

The "k" in Afrikan shows that this is a book of Eddie Murphism, a list of African names meant for African American babies born to couples named Wayne and Dolores. Strange how so many Blackademe publishers have box number addresses only.

Children of the Sun, George Wells Parker. Originally published by the Hamitic League of the World 1918. Reprinted 1981 by Black Classic Press P.O Box 13414-1E Ballinport, Maryland 21203.

A unique early example of Blackademe, this book seems to be one of the inspirations for Leonard Jefferies' series of lectures. Whatever happened to the Hamitic League of the World?

Global Afrikan Presence — Reparation, Resistance Repatriation, Edward Scobie 1994. Another Blackademe publication from A&B Publishers of Brooklyn, who are getting to be a perfect pest.

Wonderful adventures of Mrs Seacole in Many Lands by herself. Originally published by James Blackwood in 1857, now reprinted by Falling Wall Press, 1984, and edited by Ziggi Alexander and Audrey Dewjee.

Like MacRitchie's *Ancient Britons*, this is a lively well-written book that owes its reissue to Blackademe — in this case of the English Hidden Black Presence variety. Along with Peter Fryer's *Staying*

Power, this book made a sensation among black readers in Britain.

Plucky Mary Seacole (1805-1881), a coloured woman from Jamaica, journeyed as a nurse to the Crimea, and ended her days in London where she is buried at Kensal Green. Her cheerful no-nonsense style of writing forms a contrast to the editors' contributions.

The editors rediscovered Mary Seacole in time to make her star attraction of a travelling *Roots in Britain* exhibition displayed in public libraries on a Hidden Black Presence theme. The reissued book's dust jacket notes declare it to be a "rare example of an early autobiography by a Black British woman".

Black Presence believers, who cannot have read the book properly, have made Mary Seacole's picture into an icon hung on the walls of all surviving Black Rights Centres. She is not admired for her work as a nurse, but for being a Black Briton.

A statue of Mary Seacole is to be unveiled at Toxteth, Liverpool 8, to symbolize the long established home-grown Black British community there. However, if Mary Seacole ever came to Liverpool, it would have been in a boat from Jamaica.

The Life of Henry Drummond, George Adam Smith, Hodder and Stoughton, 1902. Somewhat lengthy and prosey, this book nevertheless provides excellent background to Drummond's masterpiece *Tropical Africa*.

Heroes of the Middle Ages, Eva Marsh Toppan, George S Harrap & Co, 1914. Another wonderful history book to be reissued (with amendents) without delay! Most of the countries of Europe, together with their founders (real or mythical), are described in this attractive book. Mohammed, the rise of Islam and the behaviour of both sides in the Crusades are described with remarkable fairness, in a style which would be appreciated by Moslem children in English primary schools today.

Anglo Saxon Village, Monica Toppleman, A&C Black, 1994.

English history is sometimes regarded as a 'suspect subject' by teachers today. It is feared that pride in English history may be "racist". Some teachers are confounded and appalled by the lack of black faces in English history book illustrations.

Anglo-Saxon Village, with its attractive colour photographs provides the answer! The book shows a school party being shown round a reconstructed Anglo-Saxon village, where actors dressed as tenth century Anglo-Saxons give them a practical lesson in history. As "guests of the villagers", the children take part in Anglo-Saxon activities. Nearly all the children are of Indian origin, and bring a touch of the East to Saxon England. So the 'racist implications' of history are neatly circumvented. Two big jolly brown girls in blue jeans cheerfully manhandle a replica plough in one action-packed photograph. Full marks for ingenuity. (In quite a different mood, a history teacher might relax and take her mind off her work by reading a romantic historical novel.)

In the Heart of Savagedom, Rachel Stuart Watt, Pickering and Inglis, 1915.

A missionary wife from Northern Ireland, Rachel Watt describes the difficulties of travel into Kikuyuland (now part of Kenya) in the pre-colonial days of native porters in line. Hostile tribesmen, made wary by Arab raiders, lurk in the elephant grass. Rachel's husband, who died at his mission post, became the blood brother of a Kikuyu chief. The noble but warlike East Africans remind me, in this narrative, of Plains Indians in the USA. Settled at last in a mission house, the Watts became deeply fond of their converts and companions and seemed to regret the 'march of civilisation' represented by the railway. In those days, rhinos were definitely not an endangered species, but themselves endangered everyone they came across. There is a splendid drawing of Mr. Watt being chased by a furious rhino.

Rachel Watt declares that the people of East Africa are not savages and only convention (or her publisher) makes her call them so. I know how she feels — publishers forced me to refer to 'black churches' on a book cover, a term which West Indian churchgoers hate and which stops them from buying my book!

The Destruction of Black Civilisation, Chancellor Williams, 1987,

Third World Press, PO Box 19730, Chicago, Illinois 60619.

Lots of drawings of jet-black Ancient Egyptians in this American Blackademe classic. Apparently there is a Back-to-India movement among European gypsies, a companion in pathos with the spectacle of Black Americans trying to be African.

Since the rise of Blackademe, thirty odd years ago, there have been few good Black American writers. Everywhere, the academic mill crushes and distorts talent. John Storm Roberts and Mary Monroe, a music writer and a novelist respectively, alone compare with the great American Negro writers of the past.

One of those great writers, Richard Wright, describes in the autobiographical *Black Boy* the bewilderment and anguish he and his friends felt, growing up in the South with no history. No one ever spoke about slavery. What were they doing there, black people living in fear in a world ruled by White Terror? How had this come to be? History provides the answer and truthful history still lives in books old and new for those that seek it.